Collector's Items

Collector's Items
A Guide to Antique Hunting Across Canada

John Hearn

VNR Van Nostrand Reinhold Ltd., Toronto,
New York, Cincinnati, London, Melbourne

For Carolyn Miskolczi

Published by Van Nostrand Reinhold Ltd.
1410 Birchmount Road
Scarborough, Ontario, Canada M1P 2E7

Published simultaneously in the United States of America by Van Nostrand Reinhold Company, New York.

Library of Congress Catalogue Number 81-50744

Canadian Cataloguing in Publication Data
Hearn, John, 1920 -
Collector's items

ISBN 0-442-29701-7

1. Antiques - Canada. I. Title.

NK841.H42 745.1'075'0971 C81-094628-9

Design: Peggy Heath
Jacket Photograph: Peter Paterson
Printing and Binding: The John Deyell Company

Printed and bound in Canada

81 82 83 84 85 86 87 7 6 5 4 3 2 1

Acknowledgments

A thank you note to those people whose help, encouragement and generosity with the information they volunteered did so much to pull this book into shape: Bob Atkinson, Michael Bird, David Bradshaw, Ruth Cathcart, Bill Chater, Laurie Coulter, Norma and Dave Dykeman, Jeanne Elder, Col. Strome Galloway, Staff of Guelph Public Library, Sandra Handler, Pauline and Bill Hogan, Marsha Kalman, Anne Klein, Mary Jane Lupisch, Walter Peddle, Sally Roy, Neil Sneyd, and Geraldine and Richard Wells.

I would also like to thank Ronald Windebank for allowing us to photograph the platter on page 30 and his store at 78 Amelia Street in Toronto for the cover. Also the following people for lending us articles to photograph: Janice and Peter Griffiths, The Store Antiques, 588 Mount Pleasant Road, Toronto, Ontario (63, left and right); Dianne and Ray Horton (43, 61); Tom Keeling, Plantation Antiques, 608 Markham Street, Toronto, Ontario (18, 32); Ida and Ron Michel (38, salt dishes); Hilda Richardson (38, bowl); Marie and Fred Travell (36).

The following museums, antique stores, auction houses and individuals kindly provided photographs for use in *Collector's Items*: Michael Bird and Terry Kobayashi (88, 89, 95); Bellevue House, Parks Canada (120); Black Creek Pioneer Village (iv, 123); Chateau de Ramezay (126, left and right); Chateau Dufresne (127); The Corning Museum of Glass (15, both photographs); The Chrysler Museum (16, 17); Edward E. Denby & Associates (82, 83); Henry Dobson Antiques, Plattsville, Ontario (57, bottom right); Doulton of Canada (29); Gibbard Furniture (49); Government of British Columbia (111); Government of Saskatchewan, Department of Tourism and Renewable Resources (128); The Grange, Art Gallery of Ontario (122); Adam Haynes Antiques, Pelham Road at Fifth Street, St. Catharines, Ontario (24, bottom; 46, 50; 52; 58; 59, both photographs; 60, (left); Bill Hogan (78; 79); Irving House (112); Kirkfield Mackenzie Historic Home (viii); Laurier House, Public Archives of Canada (121); Log Cabin Museum (124); The Map Room (64); McGrath-Peddle Ltd., 32 Queen's Road, St. John's, Newfoundland (54); Laurier Museum (125); New Brunswick Department of Tourism (115, 116); R.G. Perkins Antiques, 1198 Yonge Street, Toronto, Ontario (40; 53; 56; 57, top right; 61); Royal Ontario Museum (10; 12, both photographs; 23, top; 24, top; 42; 44; 69; 86; 92); Town House Antiques, 216 King Street, St. Catharines, Ontario (20; 33, bottom; 35; 47, right; 93, right); Travel Manitoba (113); Upper Canada Village (8, 118); Waddington, McLean & Co. Ltd., 189 Queen Street East, Toronto, Ontario (19, 37, 97, 99) and Josiah Wedgwood and Sons, Ltd. (26; 27, both photographs).
Photography Credits
J. Borack Photography (52); V. Brais (118); Ken Brown (19, 37, 97, 99); Rob Gordon (53; 57, left and right; 60, right; 82); Jerry Hobbs/Paul Munck (18; 30; 32; 36; 38, both photographs; 43; 61, right; 63, both photographs); Willy Lobel (56); Ron McLeod (viii); Archie Miller (112); P.A.U. Photographic Associates Ltd. (27, top); Ron Vickers (108).

Contents

The clockmaker repairs an early wooden clock
mechanism in the Mackenzie House (1867) at
Black Creek Pioneer Village, Toronto, Ontario.

Preface

The title of this book, *Collector's Items,* reflects what I see as the present phase of collecting in Canada:

Phase One   Neglect
Phase Two   The Golden Age
Phase Three   Collector's Items
Phase Four   Museum Pieces.

The first phase, which ended abruptly in 1967, was the Age of Neglect when old pine dry sinks were treasured as kindling and when most people associated antiques only with spinning wheels.

With Canada's Centennial in 1967, the Golden Age was born — the Golden Age for the collector, that is. During this period new values were being established for articles which were still fairly abundant and still in the possession of their original owners, who were generally unconcerned about what was happening out there in the collectors' market. Those were the days when those famous little old ladies would actually pay you to cart their ugly old pine corner cupboards away; when their basements were cluttered with amber Beaver jars all facing left, which they were pleased to clear out for a dollar a bushel basket; when attics and barn lofts were yielding treasures to collectors who were regarded as crazy for parting with good money in exchange for rubbish which would otherwise have been sent to the dump.

It should never be thought that collectors of the early Golden Age were in any way swindling their suppliers. Far from it. They were in fact *overpaying* in relation to the values prevailing at that time. It was the collectors themselves who created the new values.

The Golden Age lasted no more than ten years. Its passing coincided with the end of an Age of Innocence on which it was based, and we have now entered the Age of the Collector's Item.

It is reasonable to assume that there is virtually no one in the whole of Canada who does not know that old things are worth good money. In fact, the Age of Innocence has been superceded by the Age of Unreal Expectations, and the current myth is that any old things are worth far more than reality dictates. We may assume that there are no more hidden hoards of Canadian antiques to be drawn on and that almost every attic has now been picked clean of everything that can be sold, right down to the garage sale level. Whatever those famous little old ladies choose to keep must now rate as collector's items to them too.

This, of course, is not 100 percent true, and neglected pieces will still surface from time to time, but we have now reached a classic supply and demand situation — a finite, almost measurable number of pieces, and most of them in the hands of collectors. This great non-renewable resource is now out of hiding and in the marketplace, and future trading will take place primarily between collectors, or between collectors and their dealers.

Surviving members of old families will still die, and their estates will still be sold, but it is a long time since any collector found an auction where goods were being "just given away." Gone are the days when you bought boxes of unsorted items at auction sales for $2 and discovered priceless first editions or muddily tarnished sterling candlesticks incredibly overlooked among the rest of the junk. Auctioneers are doughty men of stamina and sell their pieces one at a time right down to plastic flowerpots. They've got all day.

I offer condolences to all the new collectors. On the other hand, they may have missed the Golden Age, but they have by no means missed the boat. The total number of surviving 19th century artifacts can only diminish with time. Fire and damage inevitably take their toll. The number of collectors, meanwhile, can only go up. Time, therefore, offers an absolute guarantee of future profits, not necessarily on the extravagant scale of the past but with historical inevitability.

Time does other things, too. In terms of actual antiquity — namely being a century old — large numbers of Canadian artifacts are only now just coming on stream. All they have to do is stay in one piece in order to become 200, 300 and 400 years old. Long before that they will all have ceased to be collector's items and will have graduated to museum pieces.

The game, far from over, is already some thousands of years old and has a bright future.

The kitchen of the Kirkfield Mackenzie Historic Home, Kirkfield, Ontario. The largest crock on the table was made in Brantford, C.W., while the one on the stove is a Medalta. Also on the stove are sadirons, one with interchangeable bases. At the right is an early icebox.

1 Collectors and Their Market

The world of antiques is populated by people who view essentially the same subjects through very different eyes. There are collectors and dealers, experts and novices, those who read about antiques and those who write about them. Each develops a unique point of view.

As one of the writers, I cannot help but be influenced by all the people who correspond with me — nearly 10,000 by now. By their questions and expressed concerns, they inevitably become my most important source of information.

I rarely hear from dealers and just as rarely from experts. I would guess that maybe 20 percent of the enquiries come from collectors; the rest are from people who own some interesting old object and want to know more about it: How old is it? Who made it? Is it collectible? What is it worth?

The collectors who write to me are usually of the relatively low-budget variety. I never hear from Morton Shulman for the excellent reason that he knows more about his specialty than I do, and also because I do not address myself to collectibles in his price bracket. My mailbox is crowded with letters from people who are hungry, not for expertise, but for just a little more know-how than they already have.

Before starting this book I consulted others already published on the subject. At first glance, it might seem arrogant to pit this slender volume against the ponderous weight of all that erudition, but in fact its very lightness is its justification. When I peruse those monumental tomes, I am dazzled by a blinding display of antiques that neither I nor most other people can ever hope to own.

In other words, I am visualizing two levels of collectors; the connoisseurs and the infinitely larger number of people who are simply intrigued and delighted by lovely old things. These are the people who have discovered that it costs no more to beautify a home with simple antiques than with mail-order plastic trivia. They have also discovered that antiques can be lived with and used, as well as just looked at; far from depreciating in value, they appreciate in the course of time.

These are the people who haunt the country auctions and flea markets, decorating their homes with good taste and slim pocketbooks. The people I write for may enjoy looking at pictures of 17th century French *escritoires*, but they will probably never actually see one outside a museum. What they are going to be offered is a mass of turn-of-the-century objects and some older pieces dating back to about 1850. They will be able to acquire all kinds of interesting old chinaware, mostly ironstone, plus some Wedgwood and Royal Doulton, and mountains of Nippon and Limoges. They will see far more silver plate than silver, more pressed glass than cut, more prints than original oils. They will buy old quilts, old tools, treen and pewterware. The odds against stumbling on some neglected museum piece for $75, which is really worth $7,500 are astronomical. The odds against finding a $75 piece worth $300 are much, much more encouraging.

By far the most common theme that runs through all the letters I receive is the tenacious assumption that the information being sought does exist somewhere in some clearly stated form — that you can just "look it up" and find the answer. The hard truth is that even if the subject is limited to authentic antiques, defined as at least 100 years old, you are dealing with the survival of every conceivable man-made artifact. No encyclopedia, no matter how vast, could hope to encompass more than a minute fraction of the total information. An excellent example is Howard Pain's monumental *The Heritage of Upper Canadian Furniture*. It weighs six pounds, contains 548 pages, 1,450 illustrations, and is as comprehensive a study as you could ever expect on the subject. But I am sure that Mr. Pain would be the first to admit that it is far from complete. It covers only what is now known as Ontario; a similar book, *The Early Furniture of French Canada*, has been written by Jean Palardy, and yet another remains to be done on the Maritimes.

And that is still only furniture. Add all the books that have been written, and could or should be written about Canadian chinaware, silver, glass, textiles and every other category of artifact from the 1800s, and you are confronted with an awesome library.

For my part, I am hoping to bridge the gulf between collectors and those non-collectors who are often possessed of a number of stubborn fallacies. A common error takes the following form: "I realize that if a collector wants some special article, he or she would be willing to pay more for it than other people." A moment's thought will confirm that collectors usually pay less, not more than the rest of us. They invest a great deal of time and money in the study of their subject. They go to lots of shows, auctions, flea markets and garage sales. They read books. They join clubs where they talk with other collectors. What they get back from all this investment, apart from pleasure, is a constantly growing volume of expertise enabling them to recognize a bargain when they see one.

That knowledge is power may be a cliché, but it is also a great truth. The collector who today picks up a charming piece of Mt. Washington Peachblow glass for $1.50 at a church bazaar may have cause for self-congratulation, but it will be balanced by memories of appalling mistakes made in the opposite direction ten years ago when enthusiasm outweighed experience.

The belief that collectors have more money than sense is paralleled by the supposition that they are wildly desperate for the objects of their desire. This is not so. If collectors were rich enough, they could easily fill their homes ten times over. They are not looking for things — they can find things — they are looking for bargains!

This can be very frustrating for the non-collector hoping to sell to them. This is no transaction between equals. To achieve equality, the non-collector would have to invest a similar amount of time and trouble to become equally knowledgeable.

WHAT IS IT WORTH?

Oscar Wilde said, "What is a cynic? A man who knows the price of everything and the value of nothing." One cannot write about antiques and collectibles without readers assuming that you know what everything is worth. No matter how much you protest that you do not have the answers, the questions keep coming.

"I have in my possession an authentic widget. I know it is very old, because it belonged to my grandmother. Can you tell me if it has any value?"

This is a typical enquiry and quite unanswerable. If the question was rephrased, "How much would someone be willing to pay for it?" the problem becomes more apparent. What one collector would pay for something he or she wanted badly enough does not establish a value, only a measurement of desire at a particular time, something which maybe no one else shares.

Such questions fall into two main categories. One is, "I have a Toronto Street Railway ticket dated 1889. Is this valuable?" How can that question be answered? People do collect old transit tokens, and if they wanted this one badly enough, they might be willing to pay something for it. But how much — $1? $5? The latter figure sounds high, but not sufficiently so to class the ticket as valuable. On the other hand, it represents an appreciation from the original price in the order of 50,000 percent, a mind-boggling profit.

There must be thousands of people all over the country who have kept some such interesting memento of the past, and the same pricing problem applies to each.

In the second category is the lady from Vancouver who owns a miniature Bible dated 1629 and signed by an English Duke. Is it valuable? Although this is obviously not a $5 item, the problem is basically the same as that posed by the streetcar ticket. It has no laid down monetary value in the way that a pound of butter does and doubtless someone, somewhere, would pay a great deal of money for this little book, but, again, how much? $500? $5,000? Nearer the former I would guess. Bibles do not often achieve high prices. This is hardly a first edition, not even a first edition King James version (1611). But if the book is in good condition, and if the signer was a Duke of any importance, then there would certainly be a market for it.

The important difference is that you can afford to spend far more time and money disposing of a $500 item than a $5 piece. Not only that, but you can also afford to go to the best people in the business for help. Indeed, you cannot afford to go to anyone else. It is only the best of antiquarian book dealers who are able to locate the handful of people willing to pay $500 for a book. You should not care what their percentage is. You will still finish with far more money than you would have realized in any other way. What you are paying for is the lifetime accumulation of knowledge of the market — the most secret of all trade secrets.

*   *   *   *

I am not enthusiastic about price guides, and even less so about those that have the presumption to call themselves "official" price guides. There is nothing even slightly official about them. Mostly, they are based on surveys of American dealers who, like dealers everywhere, can be relied on to have a vested interest in reporting their highest prices in a concerted effort to establish new plateaus.

Personally, I allow for about a 50 percent swing in the reported price. If an item is listed in a price guide at $100, I assume it will trade at somewhere between $50 and $150 — closer to the former level in most cases.

*   *   *   *

I remember a woman at a show who asked me the value of a pair of rare plates she owned. I told her it was a compromise between what she wanted to charge and what someone else wanted to pay. She became very angry and said, "That's what they all tell me, but someone knows what the price should be, and I am determined to find out." She remained convinced that somewhere there was something which could be identified as a "price," although who would fix it other than the seller and the buyer is difficult to imagine.

*   *   *   *

A friend showed me a piece of unusual barbed wire; he had found a coil of about 200 yards of it in the back of a barn. According to one price guide, it was probably Allis' Flat, dating back to 1892 and listed at $10 to $15 a length. One "length" to barbed wire collectors is 18 inches. My friend, therefore, had the equivalent of 400 lengths. Does this mean his find was worth between $4,000 and $6,000?

Personally, I would not give him 50¢ for the lot — nor, I imagine, would the compiler of the price guide who could have had no idea that there were 400 lengths of it anywhere, otherwise he would not have attached such a figure to it. To preserve its value my friend should cut off one 18-inch length and throw the rest into the pond. After that, all he has to do is find out who in the world is looking for a length of Allis' Flat — and that would cost him far more than the thing is worth.

*   *   *   *

It is commonly believed that an appraisal is some kind of official price tag which attaches an indisputable value to an article. In practice, it does nothing of the kind. Your antique ruby ring may be appraised at $1,000, but that certainly does not mean you could get $1,000 for it, although it should mean that you could buy another like it for that amount. But let us suppose that your ring is stolen, and you claim the appraised value from your insurance company. The company disputes the evaluation, and you take the matter to court. Now what is your appraisal worth? It is worth precisely as much as the experience and reputation of the person who made the appraisal. If the ring was valued by the people who sold it to you, you may be in for a rough time. If the appraiser was an independent, qualified gemmologist, you should be in good shape.

There is no law in Canada requiring appraisers to be qualified in the same sense that plumbers and doctors are qualified; they are not licensed, they need pass no exam, but in practice you are no more likely to encounter an unethical appraiser than an unethical antique dealer. Integrity, however, does not imply knowledge, and it is only indisputable expertise that will stand up in a court of law.

Appraisers charge for their services. Some require a flat fee, while others work on a percentage of the total value. The Phillips Ward-Price service, to take one of the more prestigious auction houses as an example, offers a number of different kinds of appraisal: insurance, probate, current market value, division, Gift Tax, Valuation Day, damage claims, etc. Their fees are on a scale of 1 percent of the total up to $50,000 and ½ percent thereafter, with a minimum fee of $35.

*　　*　　*　　*

Dealers, in my experience, tend to be more reputable than not, but again there is no foolproof guarantee. The criteria are no different than for used car dealers or appliance salesmen. All have two main objectives: to make money and stay in business. If they are too greedy in the first objective, they are unlikely to succeed in the second.

Antique dealers are selling far more than antiques; they are selling knowledge, a vast amount of knowledge picked up over many years. The subject is so extensive that it is unreasonable to expect them to be experts in everything. They all have their own specialities. Clock people know more about clocks than anything else. The same is true for specialists in porcelain, furniture, prints, orientals, books or what have you.

My best advice is not to let dealers intimidate you. It is unlikely that you know as much about the subject as they do, but the best way of tempting them to put one over on you is to pretend to knowledge which you do not have.

Once the dealers know what you want, they will make every effort to find it for you at a reasonable price, for the very good reason that they don't want you shopping elsewhere. Like any other tradespeople, they want to keep your business and that requires them to be honest with you.

Start small. Spend a few dollars. Satisfy yourself that the goods were as represented. Then go back and tell him or her that you are pleased and spend a little more.

The idea that dealers will try to take improper advantage of your satisfaction is almost certainly false. People mostly live up or down to your expectations of them. If you indicate to dealers that you think they are crooks, they will likely provide you evidence to that effect. Mutual trust, once established, is only rarely betrayed.

One thing you may assume, what you see in the shop is what is left over after favourite customers have been phoned about the latest arrivals. Wouldn't you do the same? Wouldn't you like to be one of the people called?

Be nice. Real estate people tell me the worst thing to do when looking at a house in the presence of the owners is to deprecate it in the hope that this will bring the price down. Far better to praise it to high heaven; say how perfectly it fits your life-style, how well it has been taken care of, how heartbroken the owners must be to leave it — and how sad you are that you can't afford it. The home-owner will be open to a deal because she or he would prefer the house to pass into appreciative hands. The same principles apply to the buying of antiques.

When people ask for a "reputable" dealer they so often mean someone who will pay them more for their goods than they have to. This is asking too much. If you want to get a good price from a dealer, you should spend a little time around antique stores pricing similar items, allow for a generous markup and then tell the man what you want for them. After that a little friendly dickering ought to do the trick.

Finally, nothing astonishes antique dealers so much as to discover that people find them intimidating. Only gentle, friendly people would ever have got into such a business.

Selecting the Canadian Antique Dealers Association for special mention may be a little unfair to many distinguished dealers who are not members, but at least from the less experienced antique buyer's point of view, it is comforting to be able to identify a store which must either meet stringent standards or lose its right to display the C.A.D.A. beaver seal.

C.A.D.A. seal.

To qualify for membership in the Association the dealer must have operated an antique store as a full-time business for at least three years and every item in the store must be clearly labeled with the description, approximate date and price. There must be a descriptive invoice given with every purchase and not less than 75 percent of the stock must be "antique" — defined by the association as made before 1870.

I have evidence of memberships being cancelled through failure to meet these standards.

*   *   *   *

The most interesting of collectors are those who are also part-time traders. These are the people who have the most fun at the least risk. For them, and only them, buying and selling are critical facets of their hobby. They are the real experts; they know the field; they are acutely conscious of current prices and the wants of other collectors. They not only read the literature, they write it. Articles in collector magazines and specialist books are mostly researched, written and often published by members of this group.

Their experience is costly when measured in time spent, miles traveled and mistakes made during their early collecting years. The pay-off, finally, is a fascinating, self-financing hobby. These are the people, not just the dealers, who are first to arrive when the antique show or flea market opens. They can skim round in short

order and instantly recognize the underpriced items, acquiring them either for their own collections or for trading purposes. The rest of us get there hours later.

We need not envy them. Their ranks are wide open to anyone who wants to take the same amount of time and trouble. To them goes not just some, but all the credit for the buoyancy of today's collector market. Without them, half the dealers would cease to exist, and all those heirlooms that people write to me about would be valueless. It is the dedicated collectors who create that market and boost those values.

*   *   *   *

Glass lightning rod balls mostly date from between 1900 and 1930, after which they started being made of porcelain, and later still, plastic. There are at least 150 different Canadian balls: the familiar spherical opaque turquoise as well as amber, white, amethyst, emerald green and ruby red. They trade in the $5 to $15 bracket. The subject reminds me of the divine lunacy that occasionally possesses collectors when confronted by some inaccessible object of their desire. A couple of years ago I visited a friend who had just bought a country property which included one semi-derelict barn. High up on a still standing ridge was one remaining lightning rod ball. It beckoned me all day, until finally I clambered up the rungs of the silo, onto the eaves of the barn from whence, spreading myself as flat as I could, I wriggled over the rotting roof 80 feet above the ground and returned triumphantly bearing the lightning rod ball, which I later sold for $2.

No comment is necessary.

*   *   *   *

I thoroughly enjoyed Morton Shulman's book *Anyone Can Make Big Money Buying Art.* Morton Shulman is a rare phenomenon on the Canadian scene — someone who knows his subject and sees no reason to be modest about it. The book is fascinating and even though most of its 136 pages are filled with stories about the size of his purchases and the brilliance of his insights, it contains a great deal of sound advice which might profitably be followed, not just by those in his own income bracket, but by far less affluent collectors.

The first page of the introduction says, "If you have $500 to spend, you're in a position to start today." That wipes out me and, I suspect, a lot of my readers. On the other hand, his basic principles apply at any level:

1. Think first and foremost in terms of beauty rather than profit. The genuinely beautiful piece retains and grows in value no matter what.
2. Old is better than new. This is a matter of elementary statistics. The number of old things constantly diminishes through accident, war, fires, etc; the number of collectors and the money they have to spend constantly increases. Supply and demand does the rest.
3. Always buy quality rather than quantity. Take whatever money you can afford and buy the best with it. Next year you will have more money, then you can buy something else. Don't rush in building a collection.
4. Avoid all modern art. In fact, despite what Shulman says, if we do not buy modern art there will soon be no modern artists, but in terms of safe investment one must admit he is right.
5. Specialize. You can only develop a collection through expertise, and you cannot be an expert in everything — not even if you are Morton Shulman who certainly makes a brave attempt.
6. Buy small objects. Personal space is shrinking all the time, and fewer people have room to maintain a collection of bulky things.

For the rest he advises us not to collect today's fads, because the price will be too high, and to avoid fragile objects, erotic art and modern so-called limited editions. Buy from reputable auctioneers if you know what you are doing. Sell in the same way. Don't ever let anyone rush you into a purchase. Take all the time you need. Do not expect fast profits and plan to hold on to your pieces for several years.

One thing puzzles me. Morton Shulman and I are substantially in agreement, but if we are equally astute, why aren't we equally rich?

My best advice to any collector is: educate your own judgment of what is worth having. Develop your own eye for the good and the beautiful and then trust your own common sense. If a piece of palpable trash hits the market at what you are convinced is a ridiculously high price, you are probably right. A collection is a highly personal thing. It is to be measured by the satisfaction you get from it, not by the vagaries of the marketplace.

Another thing to remember is that it is a mistake to regard collecting as the last stronghold of the amateur. This is now a multi-million-dollar market and therefore very attractive to the nimble-witted entrepreneur.

REPRODUCTIONS AND FAKES

The Latin tag *caveat emptor* — "let the buyer beware" — has been part of every language since the declining years of the Roman Empire, when *nouveau riche* Romans found themselves owners of ostensibly authentic Etruscan antiques that turned out to be worthless fakes made in Naples and probably no more than 400 years old.

Things have only gone downhill since then, and today's buyer of antiques must thread cautiously through thickets of booby traps.

We start off with a serious problem of definition. The words "reproduction" and "fake" are sometimes used as synonyms, but this is not necessarily so. It is all a matter of intent. When a reproduction is offered as such, the transaction is an honest one. If the same article is offered as an original, it is a fake.

There is, for example, a very good business these days in modern reproduction furniture. It is sold as such, and no attempt is made to pass it off as anything other than modern. But there are crooked operators who turn these pieces into fakes by studiously battering them with chains, leaving them under the compost heap for a year and then trotting them out as "authentic early 19th century Mennonite." Again, knowledge is the key. An understanding of construction methods, types of fastenings, wood types and the patina of real age will help you avoid these pitfalls. But it is well to remember that even the square nails used in 19th century case furniture can be faked.

*   *   *   *

The quicksands that stretch out before the collector of china and porcelain are finely mapped out by J.D. Bradshaw of Stratford, Ontario, in an important letter to *CanadiAntiquer*, which he has graciously allowed me to reprint here:

> I import reproductions of 19th century English and French goods which I wholesale to the retail store trade coast to coast. They are sold as reproductions, and there is a flourishing market for such goods.
>
> I would object to any suggestion implying that dealers in reproductions are bad guys — provided they do not try to mislead people as to the true nature of their products.
>
> When I attend antique shows as a private citizen, however, I invariably see large displays of reproductions of all kinds which would lead me to believe that in this field at least, things are by no means as represented. Here is a partial list of products being sold as reproductions, any of which could easily be misrepresented, either through carelessness or chicanery: Staffordshire Flow Blue; Staffordshire prints circa 1905-1929 now back on the market with the original backstamps; copies of early Staffordshire Salt Glaze ware, Staffordshire dogs, Toby Jugs, Frog Mugs, Lustre Jugs, Hens on Nests, Wedding Bowls (all with backstamps marked "cold" and therefore easily removable, plus the crazed look so that pieces can be darkened to look authentic). Reproduction 18th century Bristol Cranberry Glass, made in Czechoslovakia, is imported in large quantities. Old Chelsea dinnerware has been on and off the market continuously since 1701, while thousands of pieces of Kent's Old Foley ware with early backstamps are imported by a network of traders.
>
> The Staffordshire region of England and the Bassino della Grappa region of Italy are jam-packed with small plants doing a landslide reproduction business. From East Germany, imports marked Dresden come from a wide assortment of factories large and small. The Capodimonte area of Italy has thousands of little operations producing 18th and 19th century pieces of porcelain artware — some of it not even porcelain but a tough plaster stone.
>
> England, Holland, Italy and the Orient are all prime sources for "antique" copper and brass reproductions. The list of producers shipping into North America would fill a New York City telephone book. Millions of pieces of Carnival Glass and Depression Glass are imported into Canada from the glass factories of Indiana, Ohio and West Virginia.
>
> The J.G. Durand Co. in France produces four million pieces of glass a day. I see dealers asking eight times the store price value for Durand's Pink Rosaline Glass Goblets. More power to them if they can get it.
>
> Recently at an antique show I overheard a reputable dealer telling a prospective buyer that Limoges was no longer on the market, because the factory was bombed during the war. Nothing could be further from the truth; in neither of the last two wars was Limoges bombed, and today there are over 130 porcelain factories and decorators producing porcelain on thousands of backstamps. People pay good money for backstamp catalogues, and most of them are a joke — importers themselves often have their own backstamps created to guard their sources.
>
> The display of antique reproductions in jewelery in the Italian trade shows boggles the brain; millions of pieces arrive in New York warehouses daily. Makers of figurines advertise their pieces as being hand painted when in fact they are areographed (spray painted and then brushed to give a hand painted effect). Eyes, lips and facial features are done with a litho process.

And so it goes on — literally impossible to keep up with!

*   *   *   *

The interesting thing about really old fakes is that they would not have been made at all except to duplicate something of great value; a first-class forgery must itself be of superb workmanship. Today, when the word "collectible" usually refers to a factory-made article, reproductions or fakes become purely a matter of economical production runs. The cost of manufacturing a few dozen Carnival glass compotes, for example, would be prohibitive. To be able to sell them at department store prices, they would have to be turned out by the hundred thousand. But if they were slipped into the antique market, just a few at a time, not at $15 each but $150 each, then relatively small runs become economically feasible.

*   *   *   *

A nice piece of fakery involves blue flower stoneware jugs and crocks — or rather crocks without blue flowers. You take an authentic century-old stoneware container, worth maybe $25, and you paint an authentic-looking blue flower design on it using an equally authentic ceramic glaze. You then refire it in a kiln, the new glaze fuses with the old and, hey presto, out comes a crock "worth" $150.

An early 19th century kitchen in Upper Canada Village, Morrisburg, Ontario. The dishes are Staffordshire blue transfer printed. Cooking utensils include a long-handled iron cooking pan on the left and an enormous collander at centre on the floor. The ladder-back chair has four square stretchers and a skin seat.

Art glass is something else again. It would be extremely difficult to pass off a machine-made product with any hope of fooling even modest expertise. The essence of the fake is that it should be cheap to make — that is in relation to the end price. Obviously $20,000 for a fake Rembrandt which is intended to be sold for $2 million would be very, very cheap.

What we do have on the art glass market is a wealth of modern pieces made by craftsmen who are every bit as skilled as those of the past. You can buy these pieces in galleries where they are as expensive as you would expect any original, unique work of art to be. Like

modern fashions, some of these may be designed along lines which were in vogue a century ago and could be misrepresented or not according to the inclination of the dealer.

* * * *

Cecil Munsey, who is the dean of writers on Coca-Cola collectibles, tells of a classy rip-off which well illustrates the state of the art.

Virtually all the cigar bands made in the United States originate from Consolidated Lithography. Their output is measured in billions, and *Fortune Magazine* ran an article about them in February, 1933. The article included an insert supplied by Consolidated showing specimens of their work, including one for Coca-Cola. The magazine currently trades for about $6. The Coca-Cola cigar band trades for $100. All you need is a pair of scissors and a gullible collector.

If you are a collector who prefers the authentic article, look closely at the bottle on the band. If the whole trademark is visible, it is probably the "real thing." If the bottle is turned a little so that you can only read "Cola," you have a *Fortune* special.

*   *   *   *

I have heard of Mickey Mouse watches trading for $100 or more, but personally I would not touch one with a ten-foot pole. Apart from the price being absurd, the problems of authentication are overwhelming. You can take any old watch from the 1930s — worth virtually nothing — and replace the face with a suitably aged Mickey Mouse, obtainable from one of the American supply houses which specialize in fake watch and clock faces and labels. It should not cost more than $1, and you have got yourself a $100 watch.

*   *   *   *

A footnote to the history of forgery; it is estimated that between 1900 and 1920, over 100,000 paintings allegedly by the great French artist, Corot, were brought through U.S. customs alone.

The worlds of art and antiques are battlefields in which the buyer, often an innocent, faces off against the forger, who is anything but. Standing between them is the expert. Experts charge a great deal for their services, but without them the buyer is helplessly vulnerable. You can afford to be philosophical about a bargain. If it turns out to be a fake, you have not lost much and that is part of the risk you take. The criminal faker knows this and frequently exploits human cupidity by hinting darkly that the item was stolen in order to account for its low price. But if you are buying some allegedly legitimate, high-priced *objet d'art*, deal only with the best.

When you come to think about it, there are no experts on the face of the earth who can prove beyond all doubt that a Rembrandt is a Rembrandt. All they can do is to subject it to every conceivable test, and if it passes them all, they have failed to prove that it is not a Rembrandt, but they still have not proved that it is!

*   *   *   *

Can you protect yourself? I think not. No clear victor has emerged in the 3,000-year-old war between forgers and experts. Most of us are neither. We educate ourselves as best as we can. If we expose ourselves to the best there is, we will be less fooled by the spurious. Deal with reputable people while remembering that they too are human and fallible, but first and last try to retain some sense of real values. While there are people around who are willing to pay $1,000 for a lithographed tin tray or $100 for a Mickey Mouse watch, you may be sure that there are other people who regard them as legitimate prey.

*Burlington Glass Works lamp in the S Band
pattern, circa 1874-1898.*

2 Glass

There are two (or two-and-a-half) ways of making glassware. It may be free blown or machine moulded. The free-blown piece is totally human in its concept and fabrication and therefore pure art. No two free-blown pieces can be exactly alike, and all that is best in glass has been made that way from the time of the pharaohs to the present day.

Pressed glass is stamped out by a machine. As an art form, it is comparable with a stainless steel sink or any other domestic artifact in plastic or metal that comes out of a machine.

Somewhere in between these two methods is the technique known as "blown in mould" — the piece is "hand blown" (a marvellously inappropriate expression) inside a mould which gives it its final shape — roughly the equivalent of painting by numbers.

Collectors of historical prints attach primary importance to the artist and possibly the engraver. The printer who churned out the finished copies like sausages is of less importance. In the world of pressed glass, all is reversed. Few designers are known by name or collected by name, and the all-important mould-makers are virtually anonymous. All the credit goes to the manufacturers.

Machine-made pressed glass was an American gift to the world dating from the 1820s. Its history through the rest of the century is included in the still scantily recorded story of Yankee ingenuity registered in one mould patent after another as they solved the problems of machine pressing even more complex shapes bearing even more intricate designs.

Mould-making was a time-consuming and extremely expensive process. The cost of present-day moulds is measured in the tens of thousands of dollars, and back in the early days of pressed glass the cost was proportionately no less. Some of the mould-makers were free-lancers who supplied different companies. Some of the larger American glass houses had their mould-makers do custom work for smaller houses that could not afford a full-time mould-making operation of their own. Moulds were exchanged between glass-makers, lent and rented out. Exactly what finally came off the production line, when, where and made by whom, was determined only by the moulds used and nothing else, and yet some study of pressed glass literature persuades me that the history of this aspect of one of our most popular collectibles has never received serious coverage.

For the collector, pressed glass is full of problems. The moulds are fine examples of hand craftsmanship, and they are not likely to be thrown away even when the pattern is discontinued. They would be kept for decades — maybe half a century or more. They can be used again at any time. Same mould, same glass maybe, same process. Is the result an original, a reproduction or a fake? Glass collectors are hagridden with this kind of distinction. The recycling of old moulds is commonplace. It always was. Back in the 1880s when it was originally made, an item would, in the normal course of events be in and out of production all the time. The manufacturer would build up his stock and stop making it for a while, maybe a year or two. Collectors will generally accept any of the pieces made during that period as authentic, but will reject contemporary pieces as "reproduced."

It was a gigantic industry, and the collector must inevitably be guided by patterns and the names of patterns; this requires pictures rather than words. The illustrations offered here are only a few out of many thousands of different patterns and designs. The collector cannot proceed very far without one or more of the

Pressed glass celery dish, in the Canadian Thistle pattern, from the Jefferson Glass (Dominion Glass) Co., circa 1916.

These pressed glass goblets, circa 1874-1898, were made at the Burlington Glass Works, Hamilton, Ontario. The one on the left is in the Buckle with Star pattern, and the one on the right is in the Diamond and Sunburst pattern.

important books on the subject. They serve as field guides enabling the collector to identify his quarry, but of the creative process behind them, little is known.

CANADIAN GLASS

Hilda and Kelvin Spence in their *A Guide to Canadian Glass*, written in 1966, sum it up nicely.

> Pity the collector of old silver; he misses all the fun of being a detective! When he turns over an old spoon the identification is right there, stamped into it — the country of origin, the maker's initials and an indication of the date. Nothing of that kind appears . . . on old Canadian glass. One must start in with the deductive process, looking for clues in its shape, size, pattern, colour and quality that may relate it directly or indirectly to some shard that has been dug out of the ground at the site of an old glassworks, some piece that has been reliably identified by persons with a knowledge of its history or source, or some piece illustrated in an old glass-company catalogue.

Much has happened to our knowledge of old Canadian glass during the last fifteen years, but the Spences' statement remains substantially true. The story has been put together, not so much by detectives as archeologists, who have continued the patient work of digging at the sites of old glassworks. We now know a lot more but still not much.

It is when glass collectors study their treasures that they become detectives, looking for something like fingerprints — the minute but tell-tale differences between what seem at first glance to be identical moulds; looking for patterns which incorporate features from other patterns — an indication of a hybrid mould; spotting tiny defects which are repeated in other pieces — evidence of origin from the same mould. In the 1840s and 1850s bottles and windows were produced, lampwares were added in the 1860s and pressed tableware in the 1880s.

In order to identify Canadian pattern glass the Spences actually advised studying books of American patterns on the grounds that if your pattern does not appear there, it might, by default, be Canadian.

Books of photographs of Canadian pattern glass are now available, and the serious collector can hardly function without one of them. Patterns are less difficult to distinguish than thumb prints, and the ability to recognize some of the standard designs at a glance is the first step towards a collection which could never be complete.

CARNIVAL

Iridescent glass popularized by such great artists as Louis Comfort Tiffany was made by incorporating various metals into the hot glass. It was a carriage trade item and remains rare and precious. The mass production of what came to be known as Carnival glass was made possible by the perfecting of a process whereby a fired-on coating of metallic salts produced similar effects at a far lower cost.

According to Marion Hartung, dean of writers on Carnival glass, its peak years were 1905 to 1925 when it sold in enormous quantities all over the continent, primarily through mail-order catalogues. It was only in its decline that it reached the carnival, premium and dime store market. The best quality pieces all belong to the early years.

Larry Freeman in his book *Iridescent Glass*, published back in 1956, says: "Cheap iridescent glass was the most popular coloured variety ever to make the American market. Though much of it was garish, it filled the fancy of a great people at one stage of their development. It is impossible to class the entire product as junk; some of it achieves very beautiful effects, and with so much of it broken and thrown away, some items are already in the rarity class. It has not, will not and perhaps cannot be reproduced."

How wrong he was!

DEPRESSION GLASS

While collector enthusiasm for Carnival glass may have peaked, the star of Depression glass is very much on the rise, and it must now rank with the most popular of collectibles. In the last few years, clubs have sprung up and shows devoted exclusively to the hobby have become more frequent.

What we now know as Depression glass was popular long before 1929, and peak production was maintained all through the Thirties. It was machine moulded, employing the cheapest of glass normally used only for bottle-making. Flaws are commonplace and are masked by patterns and colours. Unlike its predecessor, Carnival glass, which had heavily moulded ornamentation, Depression glass

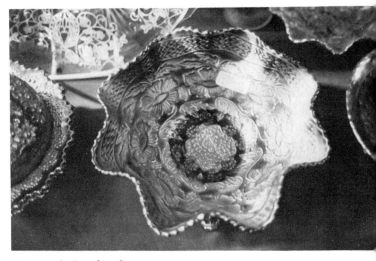

Carnival glass bowl.

Depression glass plate.

generally has a low relief pattern produced by lightly etched moulds. The effect is lacy or like snowflakes, and like snowflakes, the possible variations are endless.

Colour was determined by cost factors. Glass can be made in virtually any colour if expense is no object. Depression glass colours were limited to those which could be obtained with low-cost ingredients: for example, pink, green, milk-white and amber. Pieces retailed at that time for less than a nickel apiece and were very popular giveaway items. Through much of the Depression, Wednesday night at the movies meant two B features, newsreels, Mickey Mouse and a piece of glassware — all for 25¢.

Only a few years ago it was still possible to pick up Depression glassware at garage sales for $3 to $5 apiece. Not anymore. This is now a legitimate collector's item and prices in the $100 bracket are not uncommon. A 1980 show devoted almost exclusively to Depression glass, held in Ancaster, Ontario, attracted nearly 2,000 people on opening day. Enthusiasm shows no sign of waning.

ART GLASS

Anything that qualifies as art glass is bound to be valuable, because it is usually precisely what the name implies — a work of art in glass by an individual artist. Given its inherent fragility, surviving pieces in good condition are bound to command high prices.

Art glass is a late 19th and early 20th century phenomenon originating in Europe and emigrating to the United States with Bohemian glass-makers. It was the Bohemians who pioneered the chemistry of colour which makes art glass such a delight.

Shapes were determined by the Victorian love of the ornate and the whimsical. There was nothing utilitarian about those vases, candy baskets, tumblers, epergnes, goblets and compotes. They were free-blown original creations, each fractionally different in both shape and colour. They captured light and turned it into a Disney wonderland.

One favourite trick involving some esoteric chemistry was to make glass which shaded from one colour to another. Other glass-makers experimented with applied beads and rods; they frosted, crackled and satin-finished their products and incised the surfaces to expose different coloured layers underneath.

Here is a short checklist of American glass which may help identify some of your own treasures:

Amberina	A two-toned glass shading from red at the top to amber at the bottom. It was made from 1883 to about 1900 by the New England Glass Company.
Aurene	An iridescent gold glass made in New York around 1904. It was usually marked Aurene or Steuben.
Black Amethyst	It appears black but glows dark purple when held up to the light. It was made by a variety of companies from 1860 to the present day.
Burmese	A two-toned glass shading from peach to yellow. It originated from the Mt. Washington Glass Company in 1885.
Camphor	A cloudy white glass, either blown or pressed. It was popular with Midwestern factories in the mid-19th century.
Chocolate Glass	Also known as caramel slag. Made by Indiana Tumbler and Goblet Company of Greentown, Indiana, from 1900 to 1903.
Fireglow	Resembles Bristol glass but glows reddish brown rather than orange when held to the light. Made by Mt. Washington Glass Company, Boston and Sandwich Glass Company and others.
Mary Gregory	The name given to any glassware decorated with white silhouetted figures.
Peachblow	Originating with Hobbs, Brocunier and Company of Wheeling, West Virginia around 1883, it is lined with white and shades from yellow to peach.
New England Peachblow	Made in one layer shading from red to white, as opposed to Mt. Washington Peachblow, which shades from pink to blue.
Rubena Verde	Made by Hobbs, Brocunier around 1890. Shades from red to green.
Satin	A late 19th century art glass, acid vapour treated to produce a dull finish.
Tiffany Glass	Named after Louis Comfort Tiffany, who specialized in irridescent glass and Art Nouveau style.

Vaseline A greenish yellow glass resembling its namesake. It dates from 1870 to the present day.

FRED CARDER

Fred Carder was one of the greatest artists of the last one hundred years. Paul Gardner of the Smithsonian Institute has said, "In its early years Steuben Glass Works was a one-man operation, with Carder devising the glass formulas, designing the ware, supervising production, and dictating sales policies. New colours, classic and exotic forms, and drawings for engraved and cut decorations poured out of Carder like salt . . . " At least fifty entirely new colors and over 4,000 forms designed by Carder were introduced between 1904 and 1914. He went on to develop an equal number of colours and designs after World War I.

This is what Fred Carder said about Aurene, a type of glass he devised. "Under a microscope Aurene has many thousand lines to the inch . . . which reflect and refract the light rays, giving the iridescent or lustrous

A unique and valuable Aurene vase, circa 1905, made at the Steuben Glass Works.

Fred Carder made and signed this intarsia footed bowl at the Steuben Works in Corning, New York, about 1920.

sheen. If iron chloride be sprayed on instead of tin salt . . . a golden color is produced. The beauty of the article produced depends entirely upon the artistic manipulation of the workman."

Collecting is a hobby which operates along the plane where art and industry intermingle. All too often we do not even know the names of the great commercial designers. In this instance the credit which belongs to Carder is given to Steuben which was, and remains, one of the greatest names in glass. Yet it is not Steuben that made Carder great; on the contrary, it was Carder who made Steuben great. He was not only a towering artist, but also a formidable scientist, who brought chemical technology to bear on problems which had to be solved in order to make his creations come alive. Look for the signature "F. Carder" or the initials "F.C." He only signed pieces for which he was personally responsible.

Something of the absurdity which occasionally confounds collectors is revealed in this statement by writer John Hotchkiss. "Opinions are sometimes expressed that Mr. Carder often signed pieces which were not Steuben and therefore his personal signature should not be given too much weight." The implication is that it is more important for a piece to be Steuben than Carder, an extraordinary inversion of true values.

TIFFANY

Louis Comfort Tiffany was not just the man who made all those lamps, he was one of the great artists of modern times. He was the unchallenged leader of the art glass movement and the most important name in American Art Nouveau. He left a mighty legacy of things of beauty ranging from jewelry to stained glass windows.

Tiffany was born in 1848 in New York City, eldest son of Charles Tiffany, president of one of the country's leading silver and jewelry companies. It was assumed that Louis would go into his father's business, but instead he went to Paris to study art. He remained a professional artist until 1879, by which time he had become fascinated by the idea of bringing fine art to a wider audience through

An extremely ornate example of the familiar Tiffany lamp. This Wisteria lamp was designed in the early 1900s. (The Chrysler Museum, Norfolk, Virginia)

the utilitarian and decorative crafts. Tired of painting only for connoisseurs, he formed Louis C. Tiffany & Associated Artists, a company specializing in interior design. In short order, the company secured a number of important and highly visible commissions.

His personal interest quickly focussed on the artistic potential of glass, by no means a simple step for any artist, no matter how talented, who is not also a chemist. Tiffany immersed himself in the technological problems involved and was not long in developing the glass most often associated with him — Favrile. Pieces were subjected to metallic vapours while the glass was still hot, resulting in layers of dazzling rainbow hues.

Glass made at the Tiffany Furnaces in Corona, New York, is avidly collected by individuals and museums able to afford the hefty prices. This Tiffany cameo vase dates from about 1909. (The Chrysler Museum, Norfolk, Virginia)

Tiffany developed a strong interest in stained glass windows. He considered those made after the 14th century decadent, because window-makers began decorating the surface of the glass rather than working with solid colours. He was soon able to produce clear glass of any colour or lustre required. Another of his innovations was the outlining of figures with lead, rather than using lead to bind separate pieces of stained glass in a random fashion.

His activities continuously expanded to embrace many kinds of lighting fixtures, furniture, mosaics, enamelware, desk sets, jewelry and, of course, lamps. He encouraged creativity and insisted that every piece should be "one of a kind", despite the fact that company output grew to 30,000 pieces of blown glass in a single day.

Tiffany and modern art parted company when in his view the latter began to abandon the inspiration of nature and fall under the influence of the machine age. He died in 1933 relatively unhonoured. His Favrile glass was thought to be of little value and he was regarded as an eccentric who confused art with beauty. No one seemed to notice that when art divorced itself from beauty, it was art that died.

If current auction prices are a fair measurement of esteem, Tiffany's genius has now clearly been reaffirmed. Sotheby's sold his Laburnam Lamp for $32,000. A daffodil lamp fetched $10,000, a floor lamp in bronze with a Favrile shade featuring yellow cabbage roses went for $20,000 and four chandeliers in a row were listed for $17,000, $26,000, $40,000 and $35,000 respectively. Those are not price guide fantasies but prices actually secured during the past five years. They are by no means exceptional.

CRANBERRY

Cranberry is appropriately named for its approximation of the colour of that fruit. People tend to hate it or love it. I am one of the latter. The colour is imparted by adding small quantities of lead and gold to the vat when the glass is being made. In other words, it goes all the way through.

Mary Gregory cranberry glass tumbler.

Cranberry was first introduced in the 1860s, when it was used to make apothecary jars. Everything else followed quickly: pitchers, decanters, lamps, vases, brides' baskets, table sets, pickle castors, cruets, etc., etc. It was blown, blown in mould, and pressed; it was sold plain or decorated; and it was and still is made in immense quantities throughout North America and Europe.

The name Mary Gregory has been associated with cranberry with no good reason, other than the fact that her paintings look better against a cranberry background than any other. That, too, is a matter of opinion. She worked for the Boston and Sandwich Glass Company, and they were famous for the many different colours which they originated. Mary Gregory is credited with decorating all of them.

Her period was the 1870s and '80s, and her name has survived from among a number of talented but unknown artisans who worked for Boston and Sandwich at that time. To my knowledge, no one claims to be able to distinguish a personally painted Mary Gregory from a piece by one of her fellow decorators, all of whom worked in the same style. At one time it was questioned whether she ever actually existed, but there seems little doubt now that she did live and paint down there in Cape Cod about a century ago.

Her style was imitation Kate Greenaway: whimsical Victorian children sporting in whimsical Victorian gardens. It may safely be assumed that every piece of "genuine" Mary Gregory is outnumbered 1,000 to 1 by reproductions which have poured onto the market from her day to ours.

CUT GLASS

The collector who thinks in terms of investment tends to be guided more by market trends than anything else. But the people who make the real killings do not follow trends, they anticipate them. This requires not just money to spare but courage and a high measure of confidence in your own perceptions.

There do exist some criteria which might usefully be observed. Consider the following: a virtually lost art, a beautiful art, a fragile art, all incorporated in pieces that either could not be made today at all, or could be made only at a cost many times what you would have to pay on the antique market. That surely adds up to an investment which only needs like-minded people to create a trend.

There is nothing new about collecting cut glass, but considering the fact that a very good piece might well cost less than a rare Coca-Cola tray, it has to be rated as seriously underpriced.

Cut glass was primarily an American phenomenon. It originated in Europe, but it was not until a 17-foot fountain of cut crystal stunned everyone who visited the Centennial Exposition of 1876 in Philadelphia that its golden age began. It lasted until World War I, when a shortage of German potash used in the making of the glass reduced the business to a level from which it never recovered.

The term "cut glass" refers to flint or lead glass which has been hand cut using abrasive or lapidary wheels and then polished with jeweler's rouge. Craftsmen used a large wheel for the deep cuts and a small abrasive wheel for fine work, usually referred to as engraving. One possible cause of its later decline was the introduction of an acid polishing process, which saved a lot of hand work but with far less dazzling results. Present-day collectors are much more interested in the earlier, hand-polished pieces.

Genuine crystal is best recognized by the clear ringing tone which you hear when you tap it. If at this point you try tapping some of your nicer glassware, you will probably find that it rings melodiously and leaves you with no more reliable guide than you had before. If you are truly interested in cut glass, therefore, you must go to several good antique dealers who will positively identify some pieces for you by a professional "tap." The authentic sound will be familiar the next time you spot a possible treasure at a church bazaar.

Otherwise, it is a matter of a good eye. Genuine cut glass exhibits far more finely edged patterns than even the sharpest of pressed glass. It is also a good deal heavier. It does not take too much expertise to recognize the real thing, but recognizing outstandingly good pieces requires a very good eye indeed — and a magnifying glass. Close examination of the patterns quickly reveals an almost incredible intricacy. Cut glass pieces used to be known as "brilliants" for the good reason that the best of them sparkled like diamonds. Designs were composed of "motifs," basic patterns which were repeated and varied within an overall concept. The motifs usually comprised a finely interwoven geometry of stars, latticework, buttons and rosettes, minutely faceted to scatter light in the most entrancing way imaginable. What the connoisseur is looking for with his magnifying glass is the perfection of every fine point and line and the mastery of the craftsman who completed his complicated wrap-around design without error.

Not all early cut glass was signed. Dorflinger, for example, one of the most famous names, never signed their pieces, although the name

A *superb cut glass vase by Gundy-Clapperton Co. Limited, Toronto, Ontario.*

might be engraved on sterling stands and handles. Such famous marks as Hawkes or Libbey were minutely etched in shrewdly hidden spots, which take a great deal of finding even with a magnifying glass and much turning of the piece to catch the light at the right angle. Canadian cut glass makers include Birks, Gundy-Clapperton, and Belleville Cut Glass.

Staffordshire figures such as these would have graced many fashionable 19th century Canadian homes.

20

3 Ceramics

Nowhere is the difference between "Canadian antiques" and "antiques in Canada" more vividly illustrated than in the area of ceramics. To quote Donald Webster in *Early Slip-Decorated Pottery in Canada:* "The market dominance of English ceramics from red earthenware to porcelain inhibited the establishment of a Canadian ceramics industry to such an extent that Canada in the 19th century produced only a miniscule proportion of what it used. In some areas of production, notably the finer whitewares and porcelain, Canada never entered its own home market."

Collectors of fine chinaware, therefore, must look to imported goods, some of which were made for the Canadian market and some for world consumption. Collectors who limit themselves to ceramics actually made in this country have a very different though equally enchanting field of endeavour. There is little similarity between the eggshell perfection of Belleek and the timeless durability of Welding and Belding, but both have their charm and their armies of enthusiasts.

A history of early Canadian ceramic imports reads like an adventure story: "On the bottom of the Atlantic Ocean lie tons of 19th century pottery and porcelain intended for sale in Canada. Crates of creamware delicately painted, black basalts . . . ironstone . . . and early bone china suitable for the gentleman's table in Halifax or Montreal, all in their day were loaded aboard sailing vessels bound for British North America and committed to the hazards of the sea."

So begins Elizabeth Collard's brilliant and comprehensive *Nineteenth-Century Pottery and Porcelain in Canada.* The true collector is as much historian as pack-rat. What is thrilling about 19th century china is far less a matter of what it is now worth than one of craftsmanship and miraculous survival of a journey lasting 100 years. It was carried from

Stoke-on-Trent in Staffordshire by rackety rail lines, to Sunderland, Newcastle and Liverpool and through weeks of Atlantic gales to Halifax and Montreal and from there across the hardest country in the world to its final destination. The miracle was that any of it survived at all.

According to Collard, crates and hogsheads would be beaten loose in the hold and their contents damaged or destroyed. Vessels would limp into port with crockery that was useless to the merchants who had waited for it. Others disappeared altogether. The *Montreal Gazette* of June 5, 1834 reported nearly twenty vessels gone down since the opening of the navigation season.

No one will ever know how many went to the bottom or how many brave men went down without the smallest hope of rescue. What then is the value of that old teapot measured, not at current market prices but in men's lives? Elizabeth Collard's book is one version of our history told in terms of Spode and Wedgwood, ironstone and earthenware. It is an adventure story throwing a brilliant light on what might appear to be a mundane hobby.

Early immigrants to Canada were generally advised to bring nothing with them, to convert all their Old Country belongings into cash and buy fresh when they arrived. The thrust of the advice was two-fold: cash was far less likely to be damaged in transit and settlers without goods provided a rich market for merchants already established here.

Fortunes therefore hung on the safe arrival of shipments containing china. Particularly important were the last and the first of the season. Full gales were a disaster not only for hungry settlers, but also for profit hungry merchants. It would be a long, long winter before the next sail showed above the horizon. Equally hazardous were the first sailings of spring when enterprising skippers would take their lives in their hands, pushing through treacherous ice-floes to bring home the first and most profitable cargoes.

"With the end of winter came clearance sales in Canadian crockery shops. There were mark-downs in . . . 'leg pans' and slop jars . . . " and announcements that " 'Reduced Prices' would prevail on 'Rich Dining, Dessert, Breakfast, Tea and Coffee Services . . . ' With the melting of the snow and the running of the sap came anticipation every year in Canada of teapots and dinner plates in 'the most novel and saleable patterns of the day'."

The sap runs deep and sweet throughout Elizabeth Collard's book. Read it and delicate old china will never again remind you of fragile grannies but will echo with the raunchy lilt of Canada's colourful past.

DOMESTIC STONEWARE

Canada's earliest stoneware pottery was established in St. Johns (St. Jean), Quebec, in 1840 by Moses and Ebenezer Farrar. It burned down in 1857 and again in 1876, after which it was rebuilt across the river in Iberville. Sons of the original Farrar kept the operation going until 1927, which makes the Farrar pottery not only the first of the great stoneware factories in Canada but possibly the last, and the only one to remain in the same family throughout its life.

Factories were established in both Picton and Brantford, Ontario, in 1849, the Brantford plant first by a few months. The Picton operation was founded by Samuel Hart who ran it until 1855, when management was taken over by his uncle, Sam Skinner. In 1867, George Lazier assumed control and operated the company for the next 20 years. Throughout this period, Lazier continued to mark his containers with the words PICTON C.W. "C.W." stands for "Canada West" and usually denotes a pre-Confederation date but does not apply in this case.

The Picton plant closed down on Lazier's death in 1887, but by that time the bulk of the operation had already been transferred to Belleville, Ontario, under the name of Hart Brothers & Lazier, a company which had been

formed in 1880 and remained in business until 1925.

The most successful of Canada's container-makers was undoubtedly the stoneware pottery at Brantford. It was founded by Justin Morton of Lyons, New York, and survived many changes of ownership and three devastating fires to remain in almost continuous production until 1907. The Brantford pottery concentrated on a basic line of containers until well after Confederation, but once William E. Welding, who was an enterprising salesman, took over management, it branched out to produce a full range of household items such as bowls, teapots, pitchers and spittoons decorated in a variety of brown, yellow and Rockingham glazes. Today these are all prime collector's items.

At its peak Brantford was one of the greatest commercial potteries in North America, despite the fires which plagued it.

Changes in management at Brantford were all reflected in the names printed on the plant's products. These changes provide a handy system whereby Brantford wares can be dated:

Morton & Co./Brantford, C.W. 1849-1856
Morton & Bennett/Brantford, C.W. 1856-1857
James Woodyatt & Co. 1857-1859
Morton, Goold & Co./Brantford, C.W. 1859
F.P. Goold & Co./Brantford, C.W. (or F.P. Goold, Brantford) 1859-1865
Welding & Belding/Brantford, Ont. 1867-1873
W.E. Welding/Brantford, Ont. 1873-1894
B.S. Mfg. Co. Ltd./Brantford, Ont. (or Brantford Stoneware Mfg. Co./Brantford, Ont.) 1894-1907

Other Canadian stoneware potteries of significance include Henry Schuler's in Paris, Ontario, which lasted only until the great flood of 1883. Flack and Van Arsdale founded another in Cornwall that survived from 1868 to 1910, and there were two in Toronto: the Don Bridge Pottery of the '50s to '70s and the Toronto Stoneware Pottery of the 1880s.

These, to all intents and purposes, are all the important large manufacturers of stoneware crocks, jugs and churns in eastern Canada during the 19th century. A fairly large number

This three gallon, salt glazed stoneware crock with a blue painted flower on the front is stamped Welding & Belding, Brantford, Ontario. Circa 1867-1873.

Glass Brothers & Co. crock from London, Ontario.

of other names that appear on containers of the period are those of local potters or merchants, not large manufacturers. Those identified with the merchant's name and town are very important to local collectors and will trade for twice the going rate in their own district.

The practice of decorating stoneware appears to be a carry-over from American potters and repeats the standard designs popular in that country. Some of them are apparently finger paintings applied in great haste on a production line basis; however, regardless of the crudity of the work, they add greatly to the charm and the price of the piece.

Earlier decorations were painstakingly incised before firing and cobalt oxide powder was brushed into the incisions. This practice had been discontinued long before Canadian plants were established and replaced by the faster method of painting directly onto the unfired surface. During Goold's term of office at Brantford, there was a brief return to the incision method, and some fine examples have survived. They are very rare and very valuable.

Stylized floral designs were by far the most common. Birds are rare and much sought after. Designs which are neither flowers nor birds are so rare as to be prized above all others and command the highest prices.

REDWARE AND ROCKINGHAM

The development of a native pottery industry is determined by a number of economic factors. The ready availability of suitable clay, a concentration of skilled craftsmen working under the supervision of artists and technologists of genius, plus the proximity of a large market, combine to create irresistible pressure. Nineteenth-century Staffordshire was virtually one gigantic pottery tooled up to supply the whole world if need be — or certainly the whole of the British Empire. The Canadian market was no more than a juicy tidbit.

Canadian inland potteries were able to pick up the salt glazed stoneware container business largely because the equivalent weight and bulk in fine porcelain was a far more profitable

A 19th century Rockingham serving dish.

cargo. Add to this the cost of transporting significant loads of stoneware containers over non-existent roads or better-occupied waterways and the conditions were ripe for Brantford and other potteries to thrive for a while.

But that was only in the production of stoneware jugs, crocks and churns. Enterprising managers like Welding of Brantford made gallant attempts to make and market such table items as teapots, pitchers, bowls and mugs, but Staffordshire remained invincible. Today's collectors, however, are grateful for every attempt to establish a domestic pottery industry and surviving examples in any condition are prime collector's items.

The problems of definition and identification are great. Redware is the correct term used for unglazed baked red clay. It is also called terra cotta and is used for vases, garden fountains, fern stands and architectural features. Red earthenware utensils finished in a clear glaze are also sometimes referred to as redware. Red earthenware pieces finished in mottled brown slip and clear glazed are known as Rockingham. Rockingham and clear glazed red tableware were made in all parts of Eastern Canada.

One must inevitably turn to Donald Webster for the history of the Canadian ceramics industry, and he points out that the numerically dominant pottery-makers were not factories but small and localized individuals or family-owned operations turning out simple vessels in much the same way as they had been made for thousands of years. Red earthenware, Webster continues, "had only one advantage, the universal availability of clay. But it was the softest, most porous and most fragile of all known 19th century materials. Vessels made from it had of necessity to be heavy-walled and generally rugged but still not particularly durable."

The greater part of 19th century Canadian redware and Rockingham was unmarked and reliable identification is extremely difficult. Brantford potteries did mark much of their output and since it was slip moulded, broken decorated pieces can sometimes be matched and verified as to their source.

This spotted redware crock, circa 1860, is a fine example of country pottery.

Medalta churn from the 1930s.

POTTERIES IN ALBERTA

This has to rank with the most improbable of Canadian success stories. Ceramics are both heavy and bulky. They have to be cheap to compete, and potteries therefore must be located close to a significant market. Considerable technology is involved and a body of outstanding craftspeople and designers absolutely essential. This is definitely not a description of Medicine Hat, Alberta, in the early years of this century.

Not only was the location wrong, but the time also coincided with the collapse of almost every other old-time pottery in North America. But along came Medalta Stoneware Ltd. in 1915, and it was not long before they were employing 200 workers of whom 28 were kept busy in the art department. Medalta shipped the very first carload of manufactured goods from the West to points east of the Lakehead and continued at a rate of one a week throughout their peak years.

An outstanding and regrettably under-appreciated book on the subject was published not so long ago by the University of Alberta Press. *Pottery in Alberta: the Long Tradition*, by Marylu Antonelli and Jack Forbes is a raunchy account of a raunchy industry. It reads like the script of a play — earthy dialogue spoken by earthy Western characters. "It wasn't hard to keep employees; you just owed them money.

They weren't hard to get; they just couldn't work anywhere else." That's the way it was in the Depression years and, according to Bert Wyatt, that's how the Alberta Potteries in Redcliff managed to survive through the early Thirties. "We were getting paid every two weeks; sometimes I'd get fifty cents for two weeks work."

Richard and Jean Symonds in their book, *Medalta Stoneware and Pottery for Collectors*, list and illustrate over 400 pieces with clear descriptions of the sizes and colours. The price guide in the 1974 edition, now long unobtainable, predicted a price rise of 10 percent a year — a wild under-estimation. I would have to tip this one as possibly the most promising of all Canadian collectibles, with the following proviso.

It appears that some Medalta ware and Medicine Hat Pottery products used a uranium oxide glaze which is still emitting risky levels of radioactivity. Orange ware with a swirl pattern and ridged and swirled Matina ware should be viewed with suspicion.

WEDGWOOD

The great Josiah Wedgwood was born in England in 1730, or thereabouts. He came from a family of potters, followed their trade and became a master potter himself at the age of 29 when he started his own business. He was an authentic creative genius combining the talents of artist, scientist and businessman.

Success came early with the development of "creamware," which caught the eye of Queen Charlotte. It was soon renamed "Queensware" and led to an order from Catherine the Great of Russia for 952 pieces, each of which was lovingly hand-painted with scenes of the English countryside. The set is still on display in Leningrad.

In 1769, Wedgwood opened a new pottery at Etruria where, on the first day of operation, he personally turned out six of the tall black basalt vases by which he is, perhaps, best known. The later development of distinctive Wedgwood jasperware in greens, blues and lilac led to the production of a wide range of items which are today the most treasured of ceramic collectibles.

A limited edition copy of the Greek Portland Vase,
which was first copied by Josiah Wedgwood in the
18th century.

His most famous pieces were copies of the early Greek Portland Vase. Wedgwood was bidding for the original (now in the British Museum) at a sale, and the price went so high that his rival made a side deal with him to lend him the original if he would pull out of the contest. Josiah agreed. The fifty copies he made of the vase took over a year to complete.

His influence on pottery was tremendous, and the best evidence of his business sense lies in the fact that the company which he founded is today one of the largest manufacturers of china and earthenware in the world.

*   *   *   *

The name Josiah Wedgwood is almost synonymous with jasper, the material which Josiah developed after more than 10,000 recorded experiments. His determination stemmed from the knowledge that what he was looking for had already been discovered — and lost — by Etruscan potters well over 2,000 years earlier. He sought a white clay base that could be coloured right through its body and would fire to a non-porous finish that did not need glazing but could be polished.

Jasperware is of two basic types: a white body covered with coloured slip, or solid colour throughout. The white design of the former is made by incising the coloured surface to reveal the white base, while the latter and more familiar type lends itself to the application of low relief designs in white clay.

Low relief jasperware has been in continuous production since Josiah's time and is still made in much the same way. The white decorations are formed by pressing moist clay into moulds from which they must be lifted by hand using special delicate instruments, applied to the dampened surface of the vessel and then pressed into place with exquisite care. The whole piece is then fired, causing the fusion of design and body.

The age of 19th century Wedgwood can sometimes be pinpointed by studying the three-letter year mark incised on the back or bottom of the piece above the mark WEDGWOOD. The practice began in 1860 with the letter "O" as the last of the three letters. In 1861 it was a "P," and so on to "Z" in 1871. Then they started all over again in 1872

The Wedgwood company issued this plate to commemorate the Montreal Olympiad in 1976.

The centennial of the Royal Canadian Mounted Police, 1873-1973, was marked by a number of companies. Wedgwood created these pieces to honour the event.

with "A." By 1898 they were round to "A" again, but from 1891 onward the word ENGLAND appears along with the three letters. This system was discontinued in 1906 with the letter "I." From 1907 to 1924 a "3" replaces the first letter and from 1924 to 1930 a "4" replaces the "3." When checking your own Wedgwood, don't forget we are only talking about the last of those three letters. And don't forget that Wedgwood & Co. (1860) is not the same firm as Josiah Wedgwood & Sons, Ltd. (1769).

Wedgwood entered the annual editions market in 1969 with a series of Christmas plates and followed it up two years later with an annual Mother's Day plate. Perhaps more interesting has been the recently added annual editions of reasonably priced and outstandingly beautiful mugs, bells, Valentine boxes and Easter eggs, which are almost bound to appreciate significantly in the coming years.

ROYAL DOULTON

Doulton dates back to 1815 when John Doulton founded a stoneware works in Vauxhall, England. By the end of the century the name was known all over the world. From the earliest times the company employed fine artists such as the Barlow sisters and George Tinworth who established the design standards for which Doulton is famous.

For today's collector the name is nearly synonymous with the term "figurine," a growth phenomenon almost without parallel. The Doulton figurine is a perfect example of one of the universal verities of collecting, namely that to make it big, a collectible must by no means be unique. On the contrary, the numbers should be substantial enough to justify world-wide collector competition. The item should be small, easily displayed and demonstrate at least a modicum of artistry.

These criteria are enough to put the Doulton figurine somewhere near the top of the heap. There should be a special term for the way they are made. Certainly they are very far from being one-of-a-kind works of art. On the other hand to describe them as mass-produced would be equally absurd. "Lovingly mass-produced" might be better, or maybe "mass-crafted."

Each one starts with an original piece of sculpture — a true work of art in the highest sense of the word. From the original model, moulds are made by master mould-makers who are themselves great craftspeople. The filling of the mould with slip is performed by hand or special machines. The length of time each figure stays in the mould is meticulously monitored. The drying process is slow, the oven is controlled to the "nth" degree and the finished colouring is hand-applied to every figure by fastidious artisans. The final inspection is ruthless, and a blemished Doulton figurine is so rare as to be collectible as a novelty.

But having said all that, the fact remains that they are quite numerous and the ever upward thrust in prices is dependant more on the ever-increasing number of collectors than any significant restriction of production.

Possibly the most important annual sale of Doulton figurines is the Torex auction held in Toronto. Some idea of what is happening to the market can be gauged by the prices attained at the 1980 sale where forty of the figurines offered each sold for $500 or more.

*   *   *   *

Doulton wares have been coming into Canada almost since the company was founded. In 1956, they opened a Canadian office and are now part of a group of manufacturers including such august names as Minton, Royal Crown Derby and Ridgeway. In 1973, Royal Doulton created commemorative busts to mark the Centennial Year of the Royal Canadian Mounted Police. They represent characteristic R.C.M.P. constables, one of today and the other of 1873. It was a truly limited edition of 1,500 pairs, one of which was presented to the R.C.M.P.

In honour of Canada's 1867-1967 Centennial, Ridgeway Potteries, a Doulton company, created the "Heritage" series of china illustrated with 15 scenes of early Canada taken from famous Bartlett prints. The line has just been deleted from their catalogue and should have a good future.

Royal Adderley, another Doulton company, introduced Provincial Bone China Florals in 1967, many of which were deleted ten years later and are therefore about to become significantly collectible.

A Doulton alumnus worth watching is Roy C. Asplin of Niagara-on-the-Lake, Ontario. He sculpted several of their popular figures and is now producing earthenware portrait jugs of historic Canadians. The prices are so unremarkable that it would be surprising if they did not escalate the momment they are discontinued. To date he has done Sir John A. Macdonald, Simon Fraser, Samuel de Champlain, John Diefenbaker, Alexander Graham Bell and Laura Secord. Others are to follow. Those in white bisque are a limited edition of 1,750 each.

A pair of busts made by Royal Doulton to commemorate the centennial of the Royal Canadian Mounted Police.

WILLOW PATTERN

Some stories are worth repeating, and the legend describing the scene on willow pattern china is one of them.

The house in the foreground belonged to a corrupt mandarin. He lived there with his daughter, the exquisite Kung-tse, and a poor but honest bookkeeper named Chang. Chang's job was to falsify the mandarin's books for the purpose of tax evasion, a dubious pursuit for so honest a man.

As might have been predicted, Chang and Kung-tse fell madly in love and legend has it that their passion knew no bounds — which probably means no more than that they gazed longingly on each other from great distances. Inevitably, word of their relationship reached the ears of the scandalized mandarin who dismissed Chang and appointed a hatchet-faced harridan to watch over his stricken daughter. He barred all entrances to the estate and constructed a kind of elegant prison through which Kung-tse could wander out over the waters and through the sublime garden but return only to the ancestral home. He also betrothed her to an ancient and strangely hideous nobleman named Tai-jin.

The wedding was to take place as soon as the peach trees bloomed, and every day the forlorn maiden would wander through her sad garden watching the swelling buds in a state of great apprehension. Then one day there came floating towards her a tiny boat made from a walnut shell and fitted with a little rice paper sail on which were printed the words "as this boat sails towards you, so do my thoughts, but when the peach blossom drops from the bough, so too will your faithful Chang sink beneath the waters."

Kung-tse found this less than encouraging and hastily composed a reply, which she swiftly embroidered in her finest silk and launched on the next boat. "Does not the wise shepherd gather up the lamb which he fears will be stolen?"

Weeks went by without a reply. The peach trees bloomed and the hideous old Tai-jin arrived with a great retinue of revellers to claim her as his own. No one noticed the stranger who slipped through the doors with the rest of the merrymakers.

The eyes of the lovers met. There was a flash of recognition followed by hours of impatience while the joyous throng dropped one by one over their cups until finally, when the last one fell asleep, Kung-tse and Chang, hand in hand, slipped through the great lacquered doors.

But they were observed and the pursuit began.

Willow pattern platter.

What we see in the willow pattern are three figures on the bridge. The first, Kung-tse carries a distaff, symbol of virginity; the second is Chang, carrying the lady's jewel box, followed by the mandarin wielding a whip. But the lovers were young and both the mandarin and the hideous Tai-jin, following behind, collapsed under the combined effects of exhaustion, wine and rage.

Tai-jin vowed revenge claiming that Chang had stolen the jewels and would have to be put to death. Kung-tse would also have to die unless she obeyed her father's wishes. The happy couple, meanwhile, were well hidden in the little house which can be seen on the other side of the river.

They were secretly married but, alas, after a few short months of bliss they were betrayed. An armed raid was made on the island from which they escaped only after the most improbable of adventures and lived securely for many years in a little village by the sea. But eventually the relentless Tai-jin tracked them down. His henchmen set fire to the house. Chang was run through with a spear and Kung-tse, in despair, flung herself into the flames.

Thus the story of the willow pattern. The gods, outraged by Tai-jin's conduct, visited upon him a revenge so terrible that none have ever dared record it, while the young lovers were turned into doves, which we see forever winging above the idyllic scene.

Even sadder than this story is the fact that it was a pure invention written to "explain" the willow pattern. It originated, not in China, but in the Caughley porcelain factory in Shropshire, England, around 1790. It must surely be the most popular pattern ever devised.

IRONSTONE

Ironstone china was first introduced by Charles Mason in 1813. Present-day marketing experts could not have come up with a better name. It was developed in response to the competitive edge achieved by the somewhat delicate but attractively decorated imports from the Orient; the challenge was to come up with something of comparable elegance but greater durability.

The Masons worked on the problem for a long time. Back in 1804, Miles Mason was advertising a British-made product as "more durable and not so liable to snip at the edges." Nine years later Charles took out his patent for Ironstone, a trade name which embraced all that was most desirable in toughness and beauty. But what was ironstone?

According to the patent, the key ingredient was 20 percent Prepared Ironstone, a finely ground slag which was left behind after processing iron ore. It sounds reasonable enough, but 150 or so years later, Geoffrey Godden, the distinguished authority on china and porcelain, had one of Mason's ironstone dishes analysed chemically. The nearest thing to iron they discovered was less than 5 percent ferric oxide. Silica and alum made up 95 percent of the total ingredients. Godden claims that the product described in the patent would never have made a workable ceramic body. It must therefore be regarded as a misleading front, registered with the deliberate intention of confusing the competition and buying valuable time while Mason gained a stranglehold on this lucrative market.

Eventually, others realized they were being misled and soon both Spode and Ridgeway were producing their own ironstone dinnerware. The interesting thing is that ironstone is clumsy stuff, and by no stretch of the imagination could it be considered competitive with fragile Oriental china. But Ironstone's ability to stand up to brutal travel over the unpaved roads of the wilder parts of the Empire assured its universal popularity.

GOSS HERALDIC CHINA

There is a legend that Anna's friend, the King of Siam, spotted an assortment of Goss Heraldic China in a Bangkok store. All the pieces bore the Siamese coat of arms. He promptly bought the entire stock, and to make sure that he would have no competition from other Siamese collectors, he passed a law prohibiting further sales of Goss china in that country.

Goss china is a perfect collectible, at least for the English collector, although it is extremely popular in Canada and throughout the rest of

Three pieces of Goss Heraldic China.

the world. The company was founded by William Henry Goss, who was born in 1833, and became chief artist for the Spode company before he was 25. It was then he started his own firm, and during the next 30 years built himself an outstanding reputation for his fine porcelain.

In the early 1880s, his son, Adolphus, launched the mass-produced heraldic line which became Goss China as we know it today. Adolphus traveled all over Britain sketching local antiquities, which he then made in miniature, complete with their own coats of arms. In each locality he set up one exclusive agent for the product, and eventually there was not a town of any size anywhere without its own Goss china store.

Even though the line was mass-produced, the pieces were made of the same fine quality porcelain as the best of the regular Goss line and decorated with the same secret formula enamels for which they were famous. The timing was perfect, because its release coincided with the rise of the new cycling craze, and collectors would pedal from town to town eventually filling their china cabinets with these pretty little mementos of their travels.

There was only one problem, and it throws an interesting light on the marketing know-how of those far-off innocent days. Each town had only one Goss agent, and in any sizable place there was no way of knowing who it was or where he could be found. Goss collectors pleaded with the company to publish a directory, but they just couldn't be bothered. Eventually, a private collector by the name of Jarvis compiled his own list of authorized agents with their addresses in virtually every town in the country. It was a big undertaking, and the book was an instant best seller. At long last, Goss grudgingly co-operated with Jarvis to keep his records up to date. *The Goss Record,* as it was called, continued to be published until 1921, and it is a collector's item in its own right today. Just how many different Goss miniatures were issued is unknown, but the number probably exceeds 7,000, enough to keep the most acquisitive of cyclists and collectors busy for a very long time.

In 1893, the company introduced a new and highly successful line of coloured porcelain models of famous buildings. These are now known as "cottages" and are eagerly sought by collectors at prices running to some thousands of dollars. The mantle of the long-gone Mr. Jarvis seems to have fallen onto a gentleman by the name of Nicholas Pine, who publishes a magazine for Goss collectors and a reasonably comprehensive price guide. His address will be found in the Bibliography under Ceramics.

FLOW BLUE

Flow Blue dates back to around 1833, when it was discovered that the cobalt used to produce the blue colour on chinaware could be persuaded to blur and run if lime or ammonia was added to the kiln. I have the feeling that this was one of those mistakes which in the ordinary way would have resulted in the batch being destroyed, but some enterprising salesman sold the result as seconds and found he had a winner. There is, alas, no evidence to support this story, but its plausibility must be admitted. The softening of the line, which everyone found so attractive, also had the advantage of masking mistakes. The blue colouring of the back of each plate does not come from the bleeding through of the pigment but by transfer from the wet plate stacked underneath it in the kiln.

Pieces marked FLOW BLUE on the reverse side are almost certainly of recent

Three excellent pieces of English spatterware manufactured for the American market during the 19th century.

manufacture. In fact, the reverse side should have no mark other than the maker's name. By the time it was required to mark pieces with the name of the country of origin, the Flow Blue craze, dating roughly from 1840 to 1885, was well past its peak. Flow Blue is popular with furniture collectors, because it was made at about the same time as a great many Maritime, Quebec and Ontario cupboards. They complement each other nicely.

PORT NEUF

In the early part of the 19th century, Stoke-on-Trent potteries in England began to export a cheap line of chinaware to working class consumers in North America. Spatterware, as

Flow Blue patterns were made by a variety of companies during the 19th century. This example is called "Water Nymph" and was exported by Wedgwood.

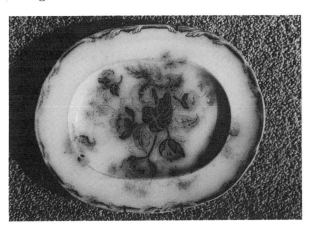

its name implies, is a ceramic which has been decorated by tapping dry pigment over the damp surface of the pieces before glazing. Designs were made by using stencils or by masking out areas. Pigment might also be dabbed on using feathers, little pieces of fur, soft rags or the decorator's fingers. The results were often very interesting. No two pieces are exactly alike, and makers apparently used whatever colours were available, often with bizarre effect. As a rule, a plate would be spattered around the perimeter, and the centre decorated with a hand-painted pea-hen or a transfer design of some kind, such as a cow.

More interesting is the sister art of spongeware. Again the treatment is crude. Instead of spattering with a mahlstick, the design was applied with what is always referred to as "cut sponge root," no example of which has ever been found. In its heyday it was known as "the secret art from Scotland," presumably Kirkcaldy where a lot of it was made. The effect was something like a potato cut, a very simple device cut from the cross section of a sponge root which could absorb enough pigment for maybe a dozen repeated dabs. No two shapes could be the same and no two successive dabs ever left the same amount of pigment. The results were even more charming than spatterware.

Spongeware was so popular with residents of the Port Neuf district of Quebec during the third quarter of the 19th century that later researchers came to believe that it was made there. The legend persisted until R.W. Finlayson published his book *Portneuf Pottery and Other Early Wares* in 1972, laying the legend to rest once and for all, but the name had come to stay.

Collectors who insist on mint condition may have to give up on Port Neuf. It was never "best" chinaware, and pieces without chips or cracks are virtually nonexistent. Mint or not, its folk art quality is very fetching. The prices are high; $250 for a near-perfect mug with an animal design would not be unusual at an auction.

STILL GOING STRONG

It is worth remembering that some of the greatest names in antique chinaware are still very much in business. The collector has little choice but to become something of a detective as far as identifying marks are concerned. There are excellent books on china and porcelain marks of which Geoffrey Godden's *The Encyclopedia of British Pottery and Porcelain Marks* is by some margin the most respected. It should never be forgotten, however, that unless the marks are incised under the glaze they are very easy to fake.

The next question is who would bother to fake them? The answer is, plenty of people — the moment it becomes profitable to do so. The more the prices go up, the more economical the faking process becomes. Sheets of fake trademark decals are not too hard to obtain.

The subject already fills many books and cannot be dealt with in detail here, but the following list will give some idea of which 19th century British manufacturers are still active. The date is the first year of operation, while specific types of product names are recorded in parenthesis.

H. Aynsley & Co. (Ltd.) 1873
John Aynsley & Sons (Ltd.) 1864
William Adams & Sons (Potters) Ltd. 1769
Adderleys Ltd. (Adderley Bone China) 1906
G.L. Ashworth & Bros. (Ltd.) 1862
Barker Bros. Ltd. (Meir China) 1876
Belleek Pottery (Fermanagh) 1883
E. Brain & Co. Ltd. (Foley) 1903
C.H. Brannam Ltd. (Castle Ware) 1879
British Anchor Pottery Co. Ltd. 1884
James Broadhurst & Sons Ltd. 1862
A.W. Buchan & Co. (Ltd.) (Portovase) 1867
Burgess & Leigh (Ltd.) (Burleigh) 1889
Cartwright & Edwards (Ltd.) (Boronian) 1869
Coalport Porcelain Works 1795
W.T. Copeland (& Sons Ltd.) (Spode) 1847
Elijah Cotton (Ltd.) (Nelson) 1880

A charming display of fine 18th century Worcester china.

Crown Staffordshire Porcelain Co. Ltd. (Queensberry) 1889

Derby Porcelain Works (Royal Crown Derby) 1750

Doulton & Co. (Ltd.) (Royal Doulton) 1882

Empire Porcelain Co. (Ltd.) (Shelton Ivory) 1896

S. Fielding & Co. (Ltd.) (Crown Devon) 1879

Furnivals (Ltd.) (Royal Furnivals) 1890

Gibson & Sons (Ltd.) (Royal Harvey) 1885

T.G. Green & Co. (Ltd.) (Gresley) 1864

Grimwades Ltd. (Royal Winton) 1900

W.H. Grindley & Co. (Ltd.) 1880

Johnson Bros. (Hanley) Ltd. (Royal Ironstone) 1883

A.B. Jones & Sons (Ltd.) (Royal Grafton) 1900

John Maddock & Sons (Ltd.) (Royal Ivory) 1855

Alfred Meakin (Ltd.) (Bleu de Roi) 1875

J & G Meakin (Ltd.) (Sol) 1851

Minton (Majolica) 1793

Myott, Son & Co. (Ltd.) (Imperial Semi Porcelain) 1898

Pountney & Co. (Ltd.) (Bristol) 1849

Wedgwood & Co. (Ltd.) (Queen's Ivory) 1860

Josiah Wedgwood (& Sons Ltd.) 1769

Arthur J. Wilkinson (Ltd.) (Royal Ironstone) 1885

H.J. Wood (Ltd.) (Bursley Ware) 1884

Worcester Royal Porcelain, Company (Ltd.) (Royal Worcester) 1862

LIMOGES

Limoges fruit bowl and plate.

Limoges is one of those magic names meaning many things to many people. Some will immediately think of the famous Limoges enamels of the 15th and 16th centuries — museum pieces long since. Some will think of the first 100 years of Limoges porcelain, high art ceramics ranking with the world's best. Most will think of what might be called the Haviland years, when Limoges was synonymous with superb mass-produced porcelain, which is the raw material for the collector. A few will associate the name with today's Limoges, which one commentator described as "some of the world's most beautiful artware and some of the worst junk imaginable."

Porcelain came to Limoges in 1771 with the discovery of kaolin, a fine white clay, in the local hills. By 1840, there were 18 porcelain factories established there, and in 1842 they were joined by David Haviland who was destined to emerge as one of their most famous names. The popularity of Haviland china in Canada and the United States during the rest of the century was immense. The Moss Rose pattern for example, could be seen in virtually every home.

By 1914, production was prodigious. There were literally tens of thousands of different patterns and thousands of different backstamps. The names most familiar to the Canadian collector are Theodore Haviland Limoges China, Porcelaines G.D.A. and Limoges Elite. The quality was superb, and presumably the price was right, possibly due to the fact that minor criminals were sentenced to serve their penal years in Limoges, thus providing a significant source of cheap labour.

The quantity of output, the astronomical

number of designs and the plethora of backstamps, many of them denoting only the importer rather than the manufacturer, combine to provide a lifetime of dedicated detective work for the Limoges collector.

Between the World Wars Limoges fell on hard times. In fact, according to David Bradshaw in an article in *CanadiAntiquer*, the word "Limoges" is still a colloquialism in the French language meaning "to be laid off."

Today, Limoges has returned to its tradition of fine art ceramics (along with the junk referred to before). The district is no longer competing on the mass market. Rather, it has developed into a colony of outstanding ceramists, about 135 of them. They specialize, but not exclusively so, in miniatures. Important contemporary names are Robert Piotet, George Boyer and Roger Leclair. Their works must be regarded as virtually one-of-a-kind art, and they command some startling prices.

The collector, therefore, should think of Limoges under these quite different headings. The product which flooded North America around the turn of the century is almost standard equipment in any antique sale. Whole sets of quite lovely porcelain can be bought at prices that would make them Sunday best but certainly usable. Before and after that period the name means something to be kept locked up in the china cabinet.

CLOISONNE

The word is derived from the same root as "cloistered" meaning "keeping to its own cell." To make a cloisonne piece the surface is divided into separate areas by thin strips of metal soldered on the edge to form little "cells," each of which is then filled with a vitreous enamel. As an art form it might be compared with stained glass windows. The process is complicated and requires great skill and a succession of firings for each colour. Cloisonne pieces have been found dating back to the 5th century B.C., and some are still being made. Chinese cloisonne is considered the best, but the process is so demanding that prices for any pieces are inevitably high.

Japanese cloisonne jar, late 19th century.

NIPPON

I am not myself a Nippon enthusiast. I have grave doubts about the wisdom of collecting anything for the sake of the mark on the bottom, and even graver reservations about something which never claimed to be anything other than an imitation of something else. This is clearly a minority opinion, and the enthusiasm of bidders at any auction where Nippon is offered indicates that it is indeed a popular item.

Nippon may be defined as any chinaware, good or bad, made in Japan between the years 1891 to 1921 for export to the United States. Under the McKinley Tariff Act of 1891 all imports into the United States had to be marked with the country of origin. Japanese manufacturers politely conformed until 1921 when the American Government decreed that NIPPON was not an English word and in future those imports must be marked JAPAN.

My limited affection for this collectible derives partly from the fact that given two identical articles, one marked Nippon and the other marked Japan, only the former has any value, a fact that tends to prove the point that people are buying the mark.

A Nippon bowl and two salt dishes, circa 1891-1921.

The green "M" in a wreath mark usually indicates a good piece of Nippon.

In practice, both before and after the Nippon period, Japanese ceramics may well have no marks at all, and it takes a fair amount of expertise to tell which is which. Before 1891 no marks were required, and after 1921 many pieces were marked only with a paper label which did not survive the first wash.

One magazine article on the subject asked, "What is the best mark?" It went on to say that the green "M" in a wreath is the most common and usually indicates a good piece. Again, it is an alarming thought that serious collectors should have to look at the mark to make up their minds about the artistic merits of the piece. Finally, the mark goes face downwards on the shelf; it is the rest of it you have to live with.

Oriental potters and ceramists are among the world's great artists, but Nippon is rarely Oriental in character. It was made specifically for export to the North American market in the styles which most appealed to that market: Bavarian, R.S. Prussia, Limoges, Staffordshire, in fact virtually all the popular European and American art pottery designs.

For my money the most attractive Nippon pieces are imitation Limoges. The porcelain is excellent, and the designs indistinguishable from the originals. My problem is to justify having to pay as much or more for what makes no bones about being imitation, when I can just as easily get the real thing.

OCCUPIED JAPAN

Japan was occupied from September 1945 to April 1952. During that period the Japanese, desperate for foreign trade, churned out huge quantities of cheap chinaware. Whatever the words OCCUPIED JAPAN may mean, symbols of quality they were not. I am suspicious that there may have been a well-planned campaign to create a collectible which would not otherwise have existed. Stories were placed in American collector magazines, unverified high prices were reported and believed. At one point, someone unloaded and collectors who are now looking for the next round of inflationary increases may have to wait a long time.

I also suspect that during the Occupied Japan boom years of 1972-74, friendly Japanese manufacturers would have been only too willing to mark whole shiploads of rejects with any words, requested by an enterprising North American wholesaler, or at least to clear out old warehouses of distress merchandise they never expected to move again. It cannot be too strongly emphasized that in the wide and wonderful world of collectibles, the trademark is the easiest of all things to fake and the least reliable guarantee of quality.

HAND PAINTED

The words "hand painted" printed on the bottom of a plate should not be taken too seriously. Almost all good factory porcelain is transfer decorated. The technique was developed well over 200 years ago, and modern fine art reproductions on collector plates testify to its near perfection. A moment's thought about simple production problems will confirm the unlikelihood of anything remotely approaching hand painting as we normally understand it. It is neither necessary nor particularly desirable, and it is difficult to imagine any artist worthy of the name solemnly repeating the same design even a hundred times, let alone any reasonable production run for a commercial plate.

Yet the term is freely applied to a large number of perfectly good and not significantly high-priced porcelain. Unless it is a downright lie, some explanation is necessary. In practice the whole thing may be transfer printed except for a few dabs of paint applied by hand as part of the border design. That would be enough to justify the words "hand painted" on the back. Printed signatures on plates and vases bearing decal scenes usually only indicate the original artist. For example, Angelica Kauffmann, the late 18th century Swiss painter whose style was widely imitated, never painted chinaware. Another form of hand painting is a kind of paint-by-numbers technique involving the colouring of transfer printed outlines.

A small amount of study should be enough to distinguish between what is genuinely hand painted and what is not, but it is probably wiser to assume that the words have little or no relevance except in the case of what are clearly one-of-a-kind pieces of art ceramic.

GLOSSARY OF CERAMIC TERMS

Agate Ware — Earthenware made with different coloured clays to simulate the veining of stone.

Basalt — Also known as Egyptian Black, it is an impermeable satin-finished black stoneware made famous by Wedgwood.

Biscuit — A ceramic which has been fired only once; a piece in its pre-glazed state.

Chinaware — A generic term meaning something better than earthenware, but less fine than porcelain.

Creamware — Any light-coloured earthenware.

Delftware — Generic term for earthenware with tin-enameled surface. Originally made at Delft in Holland, it was successfully imitated by a number of English potters.

Earthenware — Any pottery which is too porous to be used without glazing.

Overglaze — Decoration applied after a piece has been glazed.

Parian — A near-white porcelain-like body, almost marble-like in appearance and finely adaptable to intricate work.

Salt Glaze — Glaze applied to stoneware by the vapour produced when common salt is introduced into the kiln at very high temperatures.

Semi-Porcelain — A marketing term meaning something less porous than earthenware and less impermeable than porcelain (see Chinaware).

Slip — Clay of soup-like consistency which can be poured into moulds, used as a dip, or applied as a decorative cover coating.

Stoneware — Earthenware baked to a temperature which reduces or eliminates porosity.

Underglaze — Decoration applied before the piece has been glazed.

A fine collection of pewter.

4 Metals

The term "metals" as it is used here refers primarily to silver, gold, pewter and electroplate. The collector who insists on an identifiable Canadian trademark will have a difficult time with the first three categories, because the number of pieces known is small and the prices are high. Electroplate, on the other hand, was manufactured by several identified Canadian companies, but excites only limited collector interest. Some stirrings in the recent auction market suggest that this may change.

GOLD AND SILVER

Goldsmiths and silversmiths have always worked within a set of stringent rules designed to protect their clients. Few buyers are in a position to know or to be able to check whether gold is 16 or 24 karat, or how far their silverware falls below the sterling level of 92.5 percent pure.

Legal control in England can be traced back to the ordinances of 1238 and 1300. They set the standard for gold at 19.5 karats and established a standard for the purity of silver that has not changed in 700 years. The second ordinance penalized anyone who sold a vessel of silver before it had been assayed by the guardians of the craft and marked with the leopard's head. This was the beginning of hallmarks. The penalty for substandard material was simple enough; the piece was confiscated and handed over to the King's treasury and the offending craftsman sent to prison for as long as the King ordained. That law remained in force for 550 years.

A statute of 1423 devoted to gold made similar arrangements with fines fixed at double the value of the substandard piece. This law was not repealed until 1953.

The Plate Duty Act of 1719 introduced a system of taxation that tempted gold and silversmiths to play games with hallmarks despite a fine of £500. By 1757 the fine was replaced by the death penalty. In 1772, however, more humane legislators reduced this to a sentence of 14 years transportation, and in 1844 it became a crime to be in possession of fraudulently marked silverware.

Between 1238 and 1973 regulations governing standards and hallmarks in England were subject to no less than 22 Acts of Parliament. The 1973 Act, by the way, for the first time in 700 years abandoned the familiar gold karat rating in favour of a decimal system measured in parts per thousand compared with the pure metal. Thus, 24 karats becomes 1,000, 18 karats becomes 750, 12 karats becomes 500, and so on. Penalties under the current Act for falsifying a hallmark, removing a mark from a previously assayed piece or even possessing a piece with a fake mark run to ten years in jail.

*   *   *   *

The uses of precious metals in 18th century Quebec have been outlined by Ramsay Traquair in *The Old Silver of Quebec.*

> Until about the middle of the 18th century, silver was in use for most of those purposes for which today we use glass or china. Well-to-do people had, for everyday use, cups, spoons, forks and dishes of solid silver and the amount which they required must have been very considerable. This silver was also an investment, at a time when interest was regarded as usury and the stock exchange did not exist. In times of prosperity the family plate was displayed upon the sideboard to the admiration of friends and visitors; in case of need it could quickly be turned into money. . .
>
> Silver was [also] a necessity for ecclesiastical vessels. Canon law requires that the sacred vessels shall be made of the noble metals . . . Only for inferior vessels such as censers, bénitiers or trays was copper or pewter permissible.

The silversmith accordingly occupied a very important place in the community. His work was in constant demand both by the Church and by the laity; he was a necessary craftsman rather than a luxury as he is today.

The first Canadian silversmiths came here from France to keep the sacred vessels of the church in good repair. The first new pieces they made were copies of traditional French Catholic designs, but with the rise of a governing class there soon developed a market for ceremonial and military silverware calling for high artistry. Until about 1750, all the important names were from French Canada — Paradis, Mailloux, Lambert, Ranvoyze — but then came the founding of Halifax and an influx of outstanding craftsmen from England and Switzerland.

Population growth in the new land was explosive: 16,000 in 1700, 80,000 in 1750, 400,000 in 1800, 2.25 million in 1850. Churches sprang up in expanding and newly formed communities, all needing ecclesiastical silver; military officers, professionals and the new wealthy all added to the clamour, resulting in what John E. Langdon refers to as the golden age of silver making in Canada." (Langdon's *Guide to Marks on Early Canadian Silver* is the standard work.)

That peak period, however, was all too brief. Electroplating, a process developed in the 1840s to coat less precious metals with a thin layer of silver, quickly made significant inroads into the domestic market, while a surge in the popularity of imported ceramicware soon left the silversmiths back where they started — with the churches, the government and the carriage trade. Langdon sums it up best: "Conditions were not ideal for the development of a craft which always best flourished under patronage."

*   *   *   *

Determining the date and location of Canadian silver according to style and decoration calls for detailed study. Hallmarks help only to a limited extent. They did not routinely include either a date letter, or any indication of the quality of the silver. Further, it is necessary to remember that craftsmen, unlike creative

This typical early Quebec fork was made by a French Canadian silversmith copying French Provincial styles. The "CDD" is the monogram of the earliest owner, the "R" is a later owner's and the marks closest to the tines are the maker's marks.

Early 20th century silverplated bonbon dish.

artists, tended to depend on their patrons, and it was often the patron who determined the style. Inevitably, early styles were primarily French and primarily Catholic, and the student therefore finds himself involved in the whole body of religious arts and symbols. Protestant churches insisted on an almost complete absence of embellishment, with the Catholic church following suit in the early part of the 19th century. Then came the Victorian era with its fondness for elaborate decoration.

Parallel trends can be discerned in domestic tableware, and the perceptive student will be able to pinpoint localities with reasonable accuracy, but only after much study. These are hand-crafted one-of-a-kind artifacts. It was not until mass-produced silver-plated cutlery became available that popular designs reached all sectors of the market.

ELECTROPLATE

Electroplated silverware is certainly collected, but evidence of really widespread enthusiasm as indicated by books, price guides or collector associations is lacking. This is curious in a way, because electroplate stands in relation to crafted silverware in much the same position as

pressed glass does to art glass. And pressed glass collectors are myriad.

In its Victorian heyday, electroplate was possibly the most representative artifact of its era. It is difficult to think of anything else more ornately embellished; much of Victorian electroplate appears to be an excursion into the fantastic.

Canadian electroplate dates from 1879 when government attempts to protect Canadian industry against American competition resulted in the setting up of a number of American plants here. Meriden Britannia of Hamilton, Ontario (1879) was the first. Other important Canadian manufacturers to look for are Wm. Rogers Mfg. Co., Niagara Falls (1911), Ontario Silver Plate, Standard Silver Company of Toronto (1895), International Silver (1922), Toronto Silver Plate, and Birks. The quality of electroplate is indicated by the following terms. A.1. denotes not less than 2 ounces of silver deposited on 12 dozen teaspoons or their equivalent. Triple Plate denotes 6 ounces and Quadruple Plate, 8 ounces of silver deposited on a gross of teaspoons or their equivalent.

Pewter plate.

PEWTER

Pewter, an alloy of tin, copper and antimony has been in popular use all over the world for the last 2,000 years. It scores high in ductility and ease of working. It stretches, bends and may be compressed into almost any shape and it can be extensively worked without annealing. Its low melting point makes it easy to cast; articles could be made, therefore, by anyone who needed a sufficient quantity to justify the acquisition of moulds — monasteries, for example, or military establishments.

In the days before stoneware and ironstone kitchen and tableware became readily available, pewter was by far the most commonly used material in the making of virtually all kitchen and domestic hardware:

plates, spoons, tankards, bowls, candlesticks, ewers all poured out of the pewterer's shop.

The metal is fairly soft and does not stand up very long to everyday wear. Even though charmingly shaped pewter objects are a modern antiquarian's delight, the old pewterers were never expected to equal the craftsmanship of the silversmith. In fact, it may be assumed that any pewterer that skilful would soon turn his hand to the more precious metal, just as, conversely, silversmiths are known to have churned out pewter utensils as a low priced sideline.

According to Donald Webster, in his *Book of Canadian Antiques*, almost nothing is known about pewterers in Canada. The metal was widely used until superceded by ceramic ware, but lacking domestic sources of tin, Canadian pewterers contented themselves with recycling — melting and recasting — British imported pieces.

Even that craft appears to have been non-existent in Canada much before 1810, and evidence of its existence is limited to the finding of a few early spoon and plate moulds and a few marked pieces of Quebec origin. One marvels today at how little early Canadian pewterers thought of their wares, only rarely did they bother to mark them in any way and the users appear to have treated pewter with about as much interest as we give to today's throw-away plastic ware. Obviously, with a five-year lifespan one did not have to think about posterity.

* * * *

The terms used to describe various metal-working processes can seem a bit arcane, and a few definitions may be of assistance.

Annealing	Softening metal by heating after prolonged hammering. Alternate hammering and annealing eventually hardens the metal.
Applied	Parts such as spouts, handles, etc., which have been made separately and then soldered to the main body are said to be applied.
Black Pewter	60 percent tin and 40 percent lead used for candle moulds.
Bleeding	The exposure of base metal through worn electroplate.
Brittania Metal	Alloy of tin, copper and antimony introduced around 1825. It resembled pewter and was later used as a base for electroplating.
Chasing	Ornamenting in relief by hammering the inside of holloware against a shaped pitch block, or any indenting of the opposite side of the metal to produce an embossed effect.
Coin Silver	900/1,000 fine.
E.P.B.M.	Electroplated Brittania Metal.
E.P.C.	Electroplated Copper.
E.P.N.S.	Electroplated Nickel Silver.
E.P.W.M.	Electroplated White Metal.
Engraving	Decoration or inscription made by scoring the metal with a sharp tool.
Fine Pewter	80 percent tin and 20 percent brass or copper.
Fine Silver	Better than 999/1,000 fine.
German Silver	An alloy of nickel, copper and zinc.
Holloware Pewter	80 percent tin and 20 percent lead.
Incised	An indented mark made by striking with a punch.
Latten	A brass-like alloy used for making moulds.
Malleable	Capable of being shaped by beating.
Nickel Silver	Alloy of nickel, copper and zinc.
Planishing	Final hammering smooth before burnishing (polishing).

The Sibley brothers of Nova Scotia are considered
to be among the best of 19th century Canadian
chair-makers. This set of eight was made about
1870.

5 Furniture

In the literature of Canadian antiques, more has been written about furniture than any other subject. The following cannot pretend to be more than an overview written in the hope of whetting the reader's appetite.

THE GRAND MASTERS

The most famous names in furniture are not those of great cabinetmakers or even great designers but three mighty men of wood who gathered together the best designs of their day, laid down specifications and published them for the benefit of others in the trade.

The first was Thomas Chippendale (1718-1779), whose book *The Gentleman and Cabinet-Maker's Director*, published in 1754 was the most

Chippendale chair from The Gentleman and Cabinet-Maker's Director, *1754. (Reprinted in 1966 by Dover Publications, Inc.)*

Chippendale design elements characterize these pieces of English furniture from the 18th century.

detailed collection of furniture designs ever published up to that time. It illustrated virtually the entire range of mid-18th century domestic furniture and was issued as a guide for the benefit of craftsmen and cabinet-makers. There were 310 subscribers to that first edition, all of whom then started to make "Chippendale" furniture. Compared to his famous successors, his pieces appear weighty and ornately carved. Mostly he favoured cabriole legs with claw feet; occasionally legs are straight and tapered but never turned. American Chippendale is significantly less ornate than its English counterparts.

The bridge between Chippendale and the second great name, Hepplewhite, is straddled by Robert Adam (1728-1792), the distinguished neoclassic architect who saw furniture as a branch of architecture and designed each piece individually, not just to suit a particular room but to occupy a specific position in that room. Neoclassicism, spanning the period 1780-1850, was stimulated by excavations at Pompeii and Herculaneum and rested on Classical serenity and archeologically correct forms in direct contrast with Chippendale's rococo enthusiasm.

George Hepplewhite (?-1786) continued the anti-Chippendale revolt and emphasized lightness, elegance, simplicity and utility. His book *The Cabinet-Maker and Upholsterer's Guide,* was published by his widow in 1788, two years after he died. Elaborate carving has almost disappeared. Cabriole legs are far less frequent, and when used at all, they are likely to continue in a single sweep into the rail. Chair backs shaped like shields, hearts or ovals are as much a Hepplewhite trademark as Chippendale's pierced splats. His decorative motifs favour urns, shells, festoons and other neoclassic devices.

Thomas Sheraton (1751-1806), whose *The Cabinet-Maker and Upholsterer's Drawing-Book* was published in parts between 1791 and 1794, completed the trend away from the weightiness of Chippendale towards a gravity-defying appearance of fragility. Sheraton appears to have worked briefly as a cabinetmaker, but he never had a shop of his own, and no furniture by him has ever been

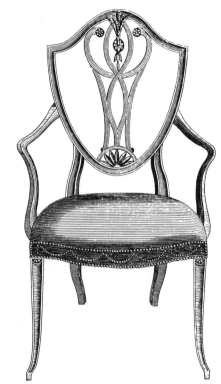

Hepplewhite chair from The Cabinet-Maker and Upholsterer's Guide, *1788. (Reprinted in 1969 by Dover Publications, Inc.)*

Sheraton chair from The Cabinet-Maker and Upholsterer's Drawing-Book. *(Reprinted in 1972 by Dover Publications, Inc.)*

identified. He taught drawing in London for a while and died in poverty as is the way of those who teach drawing. Like Chippendale and Hepplewhite, he made no bones about the fact that his book was a compendium of the best of contemporary designs, though he did add a number of original touches of his own. Square, tapered legs predominate in his pieces; turned back legs begin to appear. Lines are severe and decoration is chiefly inlay bandings. The fragile appearance of some of his furniture is more than compensated for by the superb craftsmanship. He was something of a pioneer in pieces which combined two different functions, dressing glass and writing table for example, and he made extensive use of mechanical gadgetry. All three books by the great masters of English furniture are readily available in modern facsimile reprints at little more than $10 each from Lee Valley Tools Ltd., P.O. Box 6295, Ottawa, Ontario K2A 1T4.

Around the time Sheraton's book was appearing, Duncan Phyfe (1768-1854) opened his first shop in New York City. In those days he spelt his name "Fife." He was the son of a Scottish cabinetmaker and having grown up in an atmosphere of fine craftsmanship it was not long before he was attracting carriage trade clients. All his best work, according to his own estimation, was done before 1825. During the quarter century which followed, he turned out what he himself referred to as "butcher furniture" to satisfy the less enlightened tastes of the growing class of the newly rich. It is unlikely that any of his later work enjoyed much in the way of personal supervision, as opposed to his early years when nothing left his shop until he personally had checked it out.

The motifs by which Phyfe can be both recognized and faked are the lyre with strings of brass or whalebone and an ebony key, acanthus leaves, cornucopias, plumes, branches of laurel and rosettes. He was fond of reeding, perhaps the most immediately recognizable of his devices, and liked to trim feet with brass. Duncan Phyfe is unique among American cabinetmakers in that his name, like Sheraton, Hepplewhite and Chippendale, is used to indicate a style rather than an actual maker. If present-day auctioneers are to be

believed, his output must have been prodigious.

VICTORIANA

When Victoria came to the throne, she presided over a hand-crafted economy; by the end of her reign the machine was everywhere triumphant. The first use of machinery in furniture-making took care of such preliminary work as sawing, planing and making mouldings. Then Thomas Jordan's carving machine, introduced in 1848, opened up a world of repetitive carved ornamentation while veneer-cutting machines made it possible to cover cheap furniture with exotic woods.

The Gibbard Furniture Factory in Napanee, Ontario, has been in business for over 100 years. This walnut buffet was made in the early years of the business.

Cheap fabrics from the mills of Yorkshire, and the invention of the coiled spring in 1828, led to the plushy, overstuffed upholstery for which Victorian furniture is most famous.

A huge expansion in the market for furniture of all kinds brought more and more factories into production. Population was growing at an unprecedented rate, and the burgeoning prosperity of the middle class expressed itself in a clutter of household goods that today we find stifling. One writer claims that more furniture was made during the Victorian era (1837-1901) than in the whole of previous English history.

Stylistically, the first half of the reign was a hodgepodge based on every style that had ever been. Grecian, ancient Egyptian, Chinese and Indian designs combined with Elizabethan, Medieval and Georgian were all grist for the designers' mill. The second half of her reign was marked by the conflict between the old style craftsmen and the new machine operators. This is most apparent in carved ornamentation where the hand-carvers could stay ahead of machines only by becoming ever more elaborate with their embellishments.

Towards the end of the century, we see a revival of interest in the Hepplewhite style, now nearly 100 years old. This presents a fine problem for today's collector as pieces made at that time from the original designs, using the same woods and the same quality of workmanship, must nonetheless be dismissed as mere reproductions. A troublesome thought for those who insist on authenticity!

CANADIANA

It is hardly possible to study Canadian furniture without some sense of our early history. A walk through a reconstructed pioneer village which features examples of settlers' first, second and third dwellings, tells a vivid story. The early settlers of necessity focussed all their activities on survival. Anything remotely smacking of luxury was not to be considered. Furnishings were minimal, crude and strictly utilitarian — tables, benches, storage cupboards, beds, chests — all made swiftly and simply from whatever woods came to hand.

Chair-tables such as this one, photographed in the upright position, are occasionally found in Ontario's Niagara Peninsula and fetch high prices. Circa 1835.

The moment pressures of survival eased, the desire for something other than stark utility demanded expression. Sawmills and skilled cabinetmakers followed quickly, and with them came well-crafted furniture, which is now among the most sought after of early Canadiana. Designs would still be relatively simple, but well made, and in default of carving, paint was used to add colour and life.

The third stage of society witnessed the emergence of a bourgeoisie whose prosperity was proclaimed in their homes. They imported fabrics and wall coverings from Europe but

Arrow-back Windsor side chair, mid-19th century.

Chicken coop side chair, late 19th century.

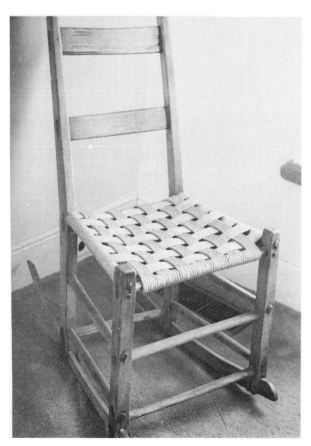

Quebec slat-back chair with added rockers, mid-19th century.

Slat-back side chair, mid-19th century.

had their furniture made by master cabinetmakers in Canada along lines fashionable in their countries of origin. To serve this market cabinetmakers had to import exotic woods and keep in touch with the latest design developments.

In the great homes of the super-successful, some of which are now restored and open to the public, we are able to see most of these phases under the same roof. The main dining, reception rooms and master bedrooms are likely to be furnished with the most ostentatious imports of their day. Children's rooms, guest rooms and possibly senior staff rooms would be blessed with the best of contemporary Canadiana — still in the European manner. It might be difficult to drag the average collector away from the kitchen and servants' quarters which remain a treasure house of pine harvest tables, great jam cupboards and a wealth of early Canadian kitchen gadgetry. Finally out in the woodshed you may still find relics of true vernacular furniture.

MARITIME FURNITURE

The Acadians came to the Maritimes in 1604, 16 years before the Pilgrim Fathers landed at Plymouth Rock. They brought chests to contain their few personal belongings and not much else. Little survives of Acadian furniture from that first harsh century, but examples from the late 1700s reveal styles which are surprisingly elegant compared with similar work in adjacent New England states. They still suggest an early stage of pioneer life with no hints of "Sunday best."

The year 1785 saw an influx of United Empire Loyalists into eastern Canada. Refugees were not able to bring much in the way of furniture, but they did not have to make the hard three generation journey from settler to establishment, and by the end of the century their influence had become a powerful design force.

Shipbuilding in the Maritimes affected

An early (circa 1800) Nova Scotia candle-stand valued at over $1,000.

cabinetmaking because the market for craftsmen was good, and specialists such as woodcarvers could take their skill from one field to another. By the end of the 19th century, the best woodcarvers in North America were centred in the Maritimes. Workmanship was of the highest order. Thomas Nisbet, a cabinetmaker from Scotland who arrived in Saint John in 1813 has been described as the Duncan Phyfe of New Brunswick. Between 1814 and 1850 his work is considered the equal of anything made on this continent.

The rise of a monied class and the lust for ostentation under the impact of Victorianism led to an enthusiasm for massively overcarved embellishment. Bigger houses were built with bigger rooms and higher ceilings, which in turn created a demand for more gigantic furniture:

huge sideboards, secretary bookcases, china cabinets and buffets, all ponderously ornamented. New Brunswick craftsmen were more than capable of giving them what they wanted. By 1870, the decline of sail in shipbuilding released more woodcarvers who had previously been kept busy working on figureheads and ornate stern boards. They now turned their skills to interior architectural features such as doors, balusters and arches.

As early as 1818 it was possible to see advertisements like the following in Halifax:

Auction of elegant furniture by Charles Hill & Co. New Furniture comprising Mahogany Dining and Pembroke Tables, elegant rosewood Card and Sofa Tables to match Hair and Canvas covered Sofas, Bedstead Sofas, Mahogany Chairs, Ladies' work and toilet Tables, Mahogany and Painted Basin Stands, Chests of Drawers and Book Cases and elegant Side Boards, Mahogany High Post and Field Bedsteads. Bedsteps etc. The above Furniture all being manufactured by the Subscriber, he can Recommend it to be of Superior Quality.

New Brunswick was an important centre for Windsor chairs made by itinerant chairmakers employing age-old methods developed in the forests of High Wycombe in Buckinghamshire, England. These combined the talents of the bodger, the bottomer and the framer whose workshop was the woods in which his raw materials were being cut down. These same ancient crafts were still being carried on in the same way in England as recently as 1950, and in the United States to the present day.

The bodger made the legs, back spindles and stretchers directly from newly split wood, which he shaped with a drawknife and turned on a pole lathe while the wood was still green. The bottomer shaped the seats and the framer assembled all the parts, a complex and highly skilled operation involving the drilling of some thirty mortise holes, gluing and wedging.

Windsor chairs come in so many shapes and sizes and designs that some definition is called for. A Windsor is any chair in which the legs, arm supports and backstays are all socketed into round holes in the seat.

Found in Woodstock, New Brunswick, this primitive two-piece pine corner cupboard dates from about 1870.

This birch chair in the Chippendale style was found in Bryant's Cove, Conception Bay, Newfoundland. Early 19th century.

Decorated washstands came into vogue during the 19th century. The Newfoundland example shown here was made from pine, spruce and fir.

A primitive pine settle from Newfoundland, circa 1850.

Walter Peddle of Conception Bay, writing in *Canadian Antiques & Art Review*, says:

> Outport, or rural, Newfoundlanders over 40 years of age are sometimes heard to say that antiques (or almost anything looking old-fashioned) remind them of "hard times." Prior to the 1940s, most outport Newfoundlanders had little money . . . they bartered their catch . . . for such essentials as clothing, fishing gear, flour, molasses and tea. Ordinarily they couldn't afford imported furnishings, so they often made their own . . . from local woods such as pine, birch, spruce, tamarac and fir. In fact, many late 19th and early 20th century examples were made from boards from demolished houses . . . parts of older furniture or even packing crates. Furthermore most of the outport furniture was built by people who were not trained in furniture construction and who were not schooled in formal furniture design techniques. Consequently, [the results] ranged from crude to fine, depending upon the skill and imagination of the individual makers.

He adds:

> There were few professional cabinetmakers even in the large populated areas, such as St. John's, and little research has been done on them, yet there was a traditional craft of furniture-making which dates back to the earliest times of settlement and continued right through to about 1940. Newfoundland did not become a wage society much before then. A small amount of furniture was imported by the late 18th century, and some was made locally by craftsmen with other expertise, such as wheelwrights, coopers and ship's carpenters. The majority of items were always homemade, because most outport populations remained isolated from commercial furniture markets. Consequently, the form, design and decoration . . . was influenced less by conventional guidelines . . . and more by the degree of skill and creativity of the individual makers.

Prosperity has yet to come to Newfoundland, but after Confederation with Canada in 1949 and the beginning of some kind of wage-earning economy, there was a massive dumping of outport furniture in favour of modern mail-order ware. Whatever is left of Canada's most authentic vernacular may still be found in woodsheds serving as storage units for fishing tackle and farming equipment.

The 18th century kitchen in the Chateau de Ramezay, Montreal. The spit in the fireplace was powered by a dog in the box to the right and above the fireplace. The early chair in the foreground has a rush seat, while the seat on the chair to its right is of woven bark.

QUEBEC FURNITURE

The process of development of vernacular furniture through three generations from the strictly utilitarian to something approaching elegance carried Maritime settlers from the English-Scottish styles of their forebears to the designs of Hepplewhite, Sheraton and the Victorians — albeit with a Canadian flair.

In French Canada the same process began with traditions derived partly from French country furniture and partly from the high styles of Louis XIII, through its own utilitarian vernacular period to re-emerge as an amalgam of the new European Anglo-French styles — again with their own distinctive Quebec flavour.

A Quebec butternut armoire in the Louis XV style, circa 1770.

This painted pine armoire from Quebec is in the Adam style. Circa 1800.

An unusual, small Quebec buffet bas, circa 1825, with original red paint.

Louis XIII furniture favoured the motifs by which French-Canadian furniture may best be identified. The lozenge, the galette or disc and the diamond points were popular everywhere. One distinguishing feature was the balancing of opposing asymmetrical panels to serve the symmetry of the whole. One sees this again and again in early Quebec furniture, sometimes as an understated allusion but more often a panache, highly suggestive of motion, which did much to diminish the ponderosity of some of those immense pieces.

The reign of Louis XIV which, after all, was longer than that of Queen Victoria and spanned the most critical years of New France, 1643-1715, had relatively little effect on French-Canadian furniture. The mock-renaissance affectations of his court, the fanciful use of exotic veneers, the delicately intricate cabinet work, the use of gold, silver, marble and a host of mythologically derived

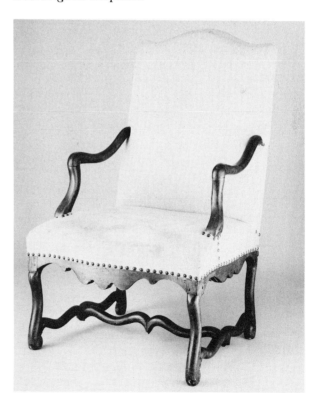

Rare furniture commands rare prices. This French-Canadian os de mouton *armchair is priced at $12,500. Circa 1750.*

decorative devices did not travel well. The forests of New France and the Courts of Versailles were worlds apart.

Changes came after the war of 1760, by which time Quebec craftsmen leapt straight from Louis XIII to Louis XV and added carved scrolls, spirals, shells and rosettes to styles and door panels. By that time, Anglo-American furniture, itself profoundly affected by Adam and Hepplewhite, made itself felt, and Quebec furniture entered the Victorian age more or less in step with the rest of the Western world. More or less, that is; the unique and fiercely independent spirit of Quebec craftsmanship remained — and remains — a visible component of everything it absorbs.

ONTARIO FURNITURE

Gerald Stevens in his excellent booklet, *Early Ontario Furniture*, written for the Royal Ontario Museum, reminds us that, "one of the earliest known items is a pine chest carved with the numerals 1796." That was 190 years after the establishment of the first Acadian colony, 180 years after the founding of Montreal, 150 years after the founding of Halifax. Just how new Ontario is, always comes as a shock.

Howard Pain points out that the new province, known then as Upper Canada, was created to receive the Loyalist refugees from the American Revolution. It is difficult for us now to visualize those thousands of square miles of bush, uninterrupted and virtually trackless, that covered the whole of western Ontario, "peopled by a scattered Indian population and a few hundred French Canadians, the only settlements a few isolated military and fur-trading outposts." From such a start it is apparent that the development of the province was one of the most astonishing performances of the 19th century. The leveling of that great forest alone boggles the mind.

To identify anything which could be described as distinctively Ontarian furniture is difficult. Lower Canada by contrast was a cohesive culture, overwhelmingly French and overwhelmingly Catholic. The United Empire Loyalists were not even uniquely British; they were Anglo-Americans, German-Americans, Dutch-Americans, Swedish-Americans,

A painted pine four-door cupboard from Lanark County, Ontario, circa 1800-1825.

Spanish, Swiss and Danish-Americans. They arrived virtually empty-handed. Jeanne Minhinnick writes in *At Home in Upper Canada* that "resourceful families brought tools rather than furniture . . . From split basswood [they] made benches, tables and shelves. Stumps often provided seats and spruce boughs served as beds."

The needs of the early settlers encompassed just about everything, and those with woodworking skills were more likely to turn them to making such essentials as window

*A set of eight Ontario gunstock chairs,
circa 1870, a harvest table and pine dry sink.*

*The number of features determines the price
of a blanket box. This piece valued at $500 is*

*distinguished by its two drawers and scrolled
bracket base. Circa 1840.*

sashes, doors, wooden pails, wooden tubs, churns, threshing mills, cradles and coffins than furniture of any kind other than the barest utilitarian essentials.

By the beginning of the 19th century, a flood of immigrants from all parts of Protestant Europe came to the new province, creating huge demands which they satisfied out of the skills learned in their homelands. Nineteenth century furniture styles in Ontario, therefore, represent a stripped-down cross section of country styles and designs popular all over Europe. Small wonder that Howard Pain's book is so massive. Nothing less could offer an even modestly comprehensive survey:

> The years from 1840 to 1867 — from the Act of Union to Canadian Confederation — were ones of tremendous growth and consolidation. Substantial houses had all but replaced the log cabins of the pioneer period, except in the most remote locations, where they exist to this day. While the early phase of settlement had been marked by courage and resourcefulness, the development era was impressive for the sheer energy involved in building the physical fabric of a new country. Domestic furnishings were obviously necessary during the early years, but the quantity required to meet the demands of rapid expansion is itself awesome in scale.

Pieces retaining their original paint are becoming more and more valuable. This small breakfront was made in Glengarry County, Ontario, circa 1850.

With affluence came the shedding of the old vernacular styles as cabinetmakers strove to offer their clients the latest in Hepplewhite, Sheraton and so on into the sophistication of the Victoria era. According to Jeanne Minhinnick, "Only the very conservative farm

This corner cupboard from Roseneath, Ontario, would be called "folky" because of its whimsical decoration. The piece is made of pine and butternut and dates from about 1860.

families preferred old shapes and styles when newer ones were offered. The ownership of old or old-style furniture had no value or prestige, and the only reasons for keeping it were sentiment, thrift, or lack of money."

She was writing about the second quarter of the 19th century. Exactly the same statement, however, could have been made any time up to 1967.

If coming to grips with all the design influences on Ontario furniture is difficult and complex, the enthusiast is at least aided and abetted by a wealth of excellent literature on the subject, virtually all of it compiled in the last ten years. Recommended titles appear in the Bibliography.

JACQUES & HAY

The transition from Golden Age to Collector's Item is marked by a certain amount of frustration on the part of new collectors when they discover that little is known about their pet interest. As a result they are inspired to don the mantle of researcher and do their own field work. One such person is Ruth Cathcart, a Toronto antique dealer who may yet have to write her own book on her subject, but in the meantime has kindly offered the following notes:

Jacques & Hay chair, circa 1860.

The reputation of Toronto's great furniture manufacturing company, Jacques & Hay, is almost as strong today as it was during its heyday in the 19th century. Auctioneers and collectors alike use their name to a point where Jacques & Hay has come to be a generic term for a broad range of Victorian Gothic, Rococo Revival, Renaissance Revival and Eastlake style furnishings — usually made of walnut but sometimes of cherry, maple or oak. This is not unreasonable in view of the tremendous output from this factory.

In its annual review of business for 1866, *The Globe* wrote of Jacques & Hay; "their furniture is distributed through the length and breadth of the land so completely that there is scarcely a house in the whole of Canada which has not some article from their workshops. Messieurs Jacques & Hay make weekly from 2,000 to 2,500 chairs and 200 bedsteads."

In addition to supplying furnishings for private homes, especially those of the privileged, Jacques & Hay completely furnished such public institutions as the Lieutenant-Governor's Mansion in Toronto and Rideau Hall, home of the Governor General in Ottawa. The company provided furnishings for the visit of the Prince of Wales in 1860, and it is said that Queen Victoria herself ordered a number of pieces from them.

Unfortunately for today's collector, they left behind no catalogues, no records of their designs, no advertisements, no drawings accompanying tenders and no labels even on the furniture they sold. Identification with any certainty is therefore difficult. An original bill of sale which stayed with the family and remained as part of that family's conviction that their furnishings originated with Jacques & Hay provides some, if not entirely satisfactory evidence. We are left, therefore, with the name of Canada's most prolific manufacturer of furniture and a serious shortage of pieces which can be ascribed to them with any certainty. The research continues.

OAK FURNITURE

Fashions in all things have a way of changing. From the days of the Pharaohs onwards, styles come and go and today's popular designs are out of date tomorrow. Fashions, however, are not just a matter of design, they also involve materials, and this is as true in furniture as it is in all other artifacts. We have just been through a period in which pine achieved the reverence that belongs only to some arboreal rarity. In other ages it was mahogany, walnut, rosewood and, of course, oak.

Oak enjoys a certain mystique because of its durability, and the table you buy today may

Oak ice box.

well last a 1,000 years, in comparison with a similar pine table which may only be good for 500 years, given the same treatment. Both ought to last for as many generations as most of us would care to contemplate.

The last few years have witnessed a surge of interest in oak furniture, especially for pieces made between 1900 and 1920 for the mail-order market. There is nothing particularly wrong with them. They were as well made as might be expected considering the class of trade and the fact that they were mass-produced. They could hardly fail to be superior to contemporary cheap furniture. Prices are climbing at a great rate, but most pieces can still be bought for less money than you would have to pay a contemporary cabinetmaker to reproduce the thing in new oak at today's prices.

I have bought oak pieces myself. They please me whenever I look at them and threaten me with internal injury whenever I try to move them. Oak is *very* heavy, as many a euphoric bidder has discovered before he ever got his latest acquisition home from the sale. Wrestling a modest oak washstand into the

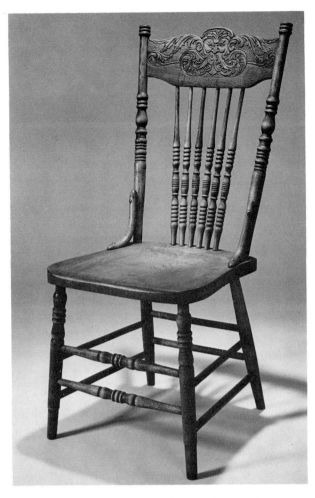

Oak pressed back chair in the North Wind pattern.

An oak fern stand.

back of a station wagon teaches you a great deal about oak.

The advisability of consulting a reputable dealer before buying is one of those platitudes which I prefer to avoid, but it is a very good idea when buying oak furniture. Oak is much favoured by reproducers of traditional styles and anything claiming to be really old needs

expert confirmation. Otherwise the usual criteria apply. You can see for yourself if it is well designed and well made, if the drawers slide nicely and do not jam or if it is split or cracked.

Do not be fooled by any suggestion that it needs minor repairs. There is no such thing as a minor repair to oak.

A treasure of early Canadian map making.

64

6 Books, Prints and Maps

If you are thinking of going in for book collecting, or are planning to dispose of all those boxes of books in the attic, here are a few basic facts to remember:

- No more than one in a hundred second-hand books is worth more than $1, and any old book that fetches as much as $20 must be regarded as valuable. Books in the $100 to $1,000 range are incredibly rare.
- "Complete Works," no matter how old or elaborately bound, are rarely valuable. The only exception may be complete works published while the author was still alive and therefore not complete.
- Valuable books fall into two main categories: first editions, special editions, finely illustrated editions or signed editions — that is of books by famous authors; and rare obsure works of special interest.
- Books containing fine prints dated before 1880, especially books of natural history and travel, may be valuable, depending on the artistic merit of the illustrations. The illustrations may well determine the actual value of the book. Two volumes of W.H. Bartlett's *Canadian Scenery*, for example, contain over 100 prints and would therefore be worth $1,000 even at a mere $10 per print.
- The vast majority of old books must be rejected purely on grounds of condition. To fetch those famous high prices we hear so much about they must be in virtually mint condition. Illustrations again are critical. If they were tipped in, one or more may be missing, drastically reducing the book's value.
- Old Bibles and encyclopedias are nearly always disappointing. The market is not good. The Bible, let's face it, is not a rare book and there is a proper reluctance to throw it away. Old encyclopedias are mostly compendiums of out-of-date information.
- The best fun for the book lover with a small budget comes from knowing your subject. I find it difficult to pass a garage sale or a Salvation Army store without going through the books, and with any kind of luck, I usually find one or two at 10¢ each which I later sell to a dealer for a dollar or more. It is a pleasant, self-financing hobby. My happiest moment was finding a 10¢ book which I later sold for $15, but that was my all-time record. Modest expectations are advised.

*　　*　　*　　*

The problem with collecting first editions is that they are not at all easy to identify. Let's see what happens.

The book is written, the type is set, the pages are run off the press and bound. That is a first edition, and if the publisher is thoughtful enough to print the words "First Edition" on one of the inside pages, it is not unreasonable to assume that this is a first — but it is by no means certain. If the type is left set up, no changes are made by the author, no new introduction written and no changes made in the illustrations or the epilogue, the next batch to be run off would also be a first edition — but a second printing. A glance at the publishing history printed inside popular books will often indicate a whole series of printings, and all of them, technically, are first editions. If, on the other hand, the type is scrapped and later reset, even though it may not be changed by so much as one letter, that printing is a second edition. As you have already guessed, collectors are not interested in first editions so much as first printings of first editions.

So far, so good. While you are scratching your head as to how you are supposed to be able to identify the difference between two absolutely identical volumes, I must inform you that worse is to come.

Old-time printing was a very human institution; automated uniformity did not yet exist. The first printing of a first edition might well be fairly experimental; the publisher might change his mind more than once as the pages came off the press — a little change here, a little change there, an illustration added, another removed, variations in the binding. It might also be discovered that there had been simple errors in the proofreading, which could be changed before the press run was complete. These errors might include misspelt words, incorrect page numbers, chapter headings upside down or any one of those ills the press is heir to.

Each of these errors and its subsequent correction is known as a point and every printing with a different point is known as a state. So the dedicated book collector is interested, not just in the first printing of the first edition, but the first state of the first printing of the first edition.

You find this nit-picking? Let me give you an example:

Tom Sawyer: first edition, first printing, first state — well over $2,000.

Tom Sawyer: any other first edition — maybe $200.

Tom Sawyer: subsequent editions — forget it.

Now you see why the upper levels of book collecting have to be approached with the meticulous care of a brain surgeon.

How does one set about getting the information that lists a semicolon instead of a comma as the only mark that identifies a first from a second state? You have to acquire bibliographies. These are catalogues listing every book, play, magazine article or pamphlet known to have been written by an author, with every edition, every publisher, every illustrator, every printing and every point itemized. Obviously such a book covering the work of even one important author will be a substantial volume, and because the market for them is small, they are tremendously expensive. Most of us

have never seen even one bibliography. They are part of the private library of any important book dealer, and he or she would not part with them at any price.

It is much easier to prove that a book is not a first edition than to prove that it is, and serious booksellers are very cautious. Even if the words "first edition" do actually appear in the book, you cannot rely on them. It may not be a first printing; it may not be a first state. In modern times when one publisher may sell the rights and the printing plates to another, the word "first edition" may well be run with the rest of it.

*   *   *   *

I am not enthusiastic about book collecting as an investment. My best advice is to do it for the joy of it. But if you must think of future profit, I am convinced that your best bet is Canadian books. Even though things have been looking up in the book world in the past few years, and preposterous bargains are less readily available than they once were, by and large, old Canadian books remain grossly underpriced.

They are attractive at all levels. If you are a $1,000 buyer, there are some superb volumes waiting for you. If, on the other hand, you have a $10 limit, you will have no difficulty in putting together a splendid library. All you have to do is to pick up a copy of any New Canadian Library Paperback reprint, and there, in the back, is a checklist of all that is best in Canadian literature. The originals can still be found in good second-hand bookstores at giveaway prices.

The mother lode, however, lies in the $10 to $50 bracket, and the shrewd collector who regularly invests in this price range will have no difficulty in building a library that should easily stay ahead of the inflation rate.

Some idea of what is available is indicated by a glance through a current bookseller's catalogue. Here are a dozen books picked at random from Pricelist #40, Patrick McGahern Books of Ottawa, December, 1980. They all date back to the 1800s and sell for $50 or less.

Alexander Begg, *History of British Columbia*, Toronto, 1894 — $35.

Daniel M. Gordon, *Mountain and Prairie*, Montreal, 1880 — $50.

William Gregg, *Short History of the Presbyterian Church in the Dominion of Canada*, Toronto, 1893 — $20.

J.C. Hamilton, *The Prairie Province*, Toronto, 1876 — $50.

John F. Herbin, *Grand-Pré: A Sketch of the Acadien Occupation*, Toronto, 1898 — $25.

Lees & Clutterbuck, *B.C. 1887: A Ramble in British Columbia*, London, 1889 — $45.

J.M. Lemoine, *Chronicle of the St. Lawrence*, New York, 1878 — $25.

R.G. MacBeth, *The Selkirk Settlers in Real Life* Toronto, 1897 — $35.

H.J. Morgan, *The Dominion Annual Register*, Montreal, 1887 — $25.

Alexander Norris, *Nova Brittania*, Toronto, 1884 — $25.

Charles P. Mulvaney, *The History of the North-West Rebellion*, Toronto, 1885 — $20.

A. Sutherland, *A Summer in Prairie-Land*, Toronto, 1882 — $50.

The possible range is enormous. Collectors are usually advised to concentrate on their own pet areas of interest. A considerable library could be assembled on such subjects as the Riel Rebellion, Canadian constitutional history, the R.C.M.P., any one of the Canadian Armed Forces, the Arctic, Inuit, Indians, rivers, churches, reformers, poets, artists or hunting. Help yourself to any facet of the social, political or military history of Canada, and a gold mine opens up that still lies within almost everyone's price range.

My best recommendation is the study of Canadian books themselves, regardless of subject. The more you know, the better you will be able to select eclectically from among the best bargains as they arise.

I do not know if the random list mentioned above represents best buys or not at this particular moment. But I am prepared to bet heavily that ten years from now the collector will look back on those prices and weep.

By way of illustration, here's what has happened to the prices of just four Canadian books since 1950:

Statistical Account of Upper Canada, by Robert Fleming Gourlay, 2 volumes, London 1822. Gourlay came to Upper Canada in 1817. A born agitator, his criticism soon incurred the wrath of the Family Compact. He was arrested, tried, found guilty and banished. In 1950, the set sold for $35; in 1960, $100; in 1971, $900; in 1979, $1,600.

Narrative of a Journey to the Shores of the Polar Sea, by Sir John Franklin, London, 1819-20. Franklin's account of his overland trips to the western Arctic, where he narrowly escaped death by starvation, is enhanced by handsome coloured plates of the Inuit and Arctic seascapes. In 1950, it sold for $30; in 1968, $95; in 1974, $195; in 1980, $500.

Canadian Scenery, by W.H. Bartlett, 2 volumes, Toronto, 1842. Bartlett, now the best-known illustrator of Canadian scenes, languished unwanted for years on dusty shelves until the revival of interest in all forms of Canadiana sent the price sky-rocketing. The set sold in 1950 for $20; in 1961, $125; in 1967, $320; in 1975, $725; in 1980, $1,300.

A Journey from Prince of Wales Fort, by Samuel Hearne, London, 1795. Samuel Hearne's account of his three overland trips to reach the Arctic at the mouth of the Coppermine River has always been admired for its typography. It sold in 1950 for $51, in 1958, $175; in 1967, $320; in 1971, $900; in 1980, $2,400.

Learning about books from books themselves is doing it the hard way. Sooner or later the collector has to take the plunge and enter an antiquarian bookstore, not a thrift bookshop or one that specializes in used Harlequin Romances, but one run by an authentic dealer in fine old books. I say this because with books as well as prints and maps, far more than any other antiquarian collectible, there is a gulf that can only be

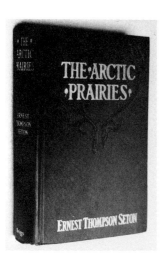

The Arctic Prairies *by Ernest Thompson Seton,* *priced at over $90 for a first edition.*

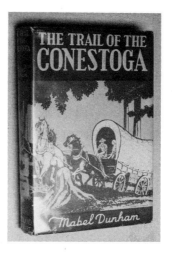

The Trail of the Conestoga *by Mabel Dunham,* *priced at over $30 for a first edition.*

Sunset Canada: British Columbia and Beyond *by Archie Bell, priced at over $30 for a first edition.*

By Canoe and Dog Train Among the Cree and Salteaux Indians *by Rev. Egerton R. Young, priced at over $35 for a first edition.*

Canadian Pictures *by the Marquis of Lorne,* *priced at over $50 for a first edition.*

spanned with the help of a good guide, and
the only good guides are the dealers. It is safe
to say that all book dealers are book lovers
who finally made a career out of the objects
of their affection. It is an affection which
they are only too happy to share.

Virtually every established antiquarian
bookseller in Canada is a member of the
A.B.A.C. (Antiquarian Booksellers Association
of Canada) and such a shop can be found in
most major cities. To be eligible for membership, one must have been actively engaged in
the business of buying and selling books for at
least three years, be recommended by four
active members and have antiquarian book-
selling as one's principal occupation. The
Association is a member of the International
League of Antiquarian Booksellers and is
governed by their regulations and standards. A
list of members can be obtained from A.B.A.C.,
Box 863, Station F, Toronto, Ontario
M4Y 2N7.

Your local antiquarian bookseller
represents only a trickle from the vast

An illustration from Canadian Scenery *by W. H.
Bartlett.*

international reservoir of books. In addition
to his or her own stock, the dealer has quick
access to virtually every out-of-print book in
the world, and rarely has any difficulty in
finding what you are looking for. The
dealer's catalogues will contain prices, giving
you some idea of what you can expect to
pay.

*   *   *   *

The mecca of the Canadian book buyer or
browser is the annual Toronto International
Book Fair, usually held in May. Over sixty
antiquarian book dealers from all over
Canada, as well as the United States and
England, offer an extraordinary display of
out-of-print, rare and unusual books, and
maps and prints, with a total value of two to
three million dollars.

Antiquarian books are not necessarily
"antique" books. They are books which are

out of print and which usually have some special value because they are rare or unusual, exceptionally fine printings, or first editions. There have been books at the Toronto Fair priced as high as $50,000, but the majority fall in the $10 to $100 range.

When Craig Fraser of Specialty Book Concern in Waterdown, Ontario, purchased Montreal Book Auctions after the death of Bernard Amtmann, he changed its name and moved its scene of operations to Toronto. Now known as Canada Book Auctions, its sales are held in St. Lawrence Hall where eight to ten times a year, about 300 of the world's best books (with a heavy emphasis on Canadiana), establish values by which other prices tend to be measured.

To have your book accepted for auction, it must be judged by their appraisers to be worth something in excess of $75. This is an arbitrary figure and may well vary according to the intrinsic interest of the work. Nor does it guarantee that the estimated price will be achieved. Their tendency is to be conservative in their estimates, and because the house commission is only 10 percent, the risk is minimal.

Canada Book Auctions does not limit itself to books. Maps, prints and broadsides are frequently offered as well as handwritten documents and diaries. Neither do they limit themselves to Canadians. A current catalogue offers such works as Dr. Johnson's *Dictionary of the English Language*, *Culpeper's Complete Herbal* by Nicholas Culpeper, a finely printed *Rubaiyat*, a number of early works on witchcraft, as well as 20 or so important pieces of Americana. Canada Book Auctions now rates with the great book auctions of London, Paris and New York. The serious book collector, even one who is not likely to be a client, might profitably send $28 a year to subscribe to their catalogue with its detailed descriptions of the books offered and the prices expected. The prices actually achieved are published later in the Canada Book Auction Record, of which there are now five volumes going back to 1967. They sell for $20 each, or all five are available for $75.

Autographs and documents are among the hottest of today's collectibles. If ever there was a seller's market, this is it. One dealer told me that collectors are "aggressive, confident and by no means lacking in funds." In certain quarters, the autograph has become accepted as a prime hedge against inflation, and as a direct and immediate result of this, prices are inflating at a stunning rate. It is necessary here to define the word "autograph." It is not, as we have been brought up to believe, the signature of a celebrity so much as an actual document, usually a letter, either handwritten or typed and signed by a person of genuine historic consequence.

At this stage the field lacks any kind of authority. By that I mean there does not yet exist any accepted body of knowledge to which the collector can refer. Nor are there any recognized criteria of values.

Such documents are not so rare as might at first be thought. A century ago almost every communication other than word of mouth had to be handwritten. There were no telephones, and no dictaphones. Letters from prominent people were always worth holding onto. We see this in biographies of the great and near great, most of which are well laced with quotes from letters that someone had the foresight to keep. Writing paper was of good quality, and so the survival rate is fairly high, but nothing like enough to satisfy all the federal, provincial and city archivists, as well as universities, historical societies and private collectors, all of whom are hungry for the authentic written word.

Among the most sought after documents in today's energetic market are the autographed letters of Canadian Prime Ministers, who become as collectible after their deaths as they were villified during their lifetimes. This is part of the Canadian way. Some idea of what is going on can be gauged by a recent offering at Canada Book Auctions:
Handwritten letter from Sir John A.
    Macdonald to Lynwood Periera, dated
    1888, 14 lines, matted and framed — $240.

Typed letter from Sir John Abbott to L.J.A. Papineau, dated 1892, 20 lines, 2 pages — $280.

Handwritten letter from Sir John Thompson to an unidentified Canadian Senator, dated 1892, 49 lines, 4 pages — $275.

Handwritten letter from Sir Mackenzie Bowell to Lt. Col. Ponton, dated 1897, 27 lines, 2 pages — $220.

*   *   *   *

Collectors of modern books and magazines must face the fact that their collections are likely to self-destruct within a few decades. Various techniques are available to prolong life, de-acidifying is one, but the process is complicated and not one for amateurs to try on their rare first editions. Experts do exist, and with any kind of luck they can be located through a good antiquarian bookstore or the librarian of your friendly neighbourhood university.

I have no idea where you would go to learn this trade. I know there are courses for art conservators at some universities, and these are bound to include seminars on the protection and preservation of paper. This is a fascinating area and well worth looking into if you are seeking a profession which is interesting, useful and rewarding. In the world of art conservation, three critical factors are constant: first, the price of great works of art, which includes books, is expanding on the scale of the outer galaxies; second, modern works of art are using an ever widening range of strange materials of unproven durability; and third, chemical pollution of the atmosphere becomes denser and more esoteric by the minute and each component has potential for adverse reaction with the paper, ink, paints or canvasses in question. One no longer measures deterioration in centuries but in weeks. The care of old books is problem enough, but the care of such things as a #1 Superman comic for which someone paid $1,000 or more is nothing short of a nightmare. Pulp magazines were made to last only until the next issue appeared. The disintegration rate is horrendous.

The work of the art conservator is an endless battle against chemical decay demanding the sensitivity of the artist combined with the pragmatism of the scientist. The job is virtually recession-proof, because even if art budgets are slashed — and they always are — existing investments are so great and require so much protection that it would be the falsest of economies to neglect them.

The same factors apply to old books. Every important library maintains a collection of virtually priceless antiquarian books and papers. They are kept, not only under lock and key, but also in specially controlled atmospheres where temperature and humidity are constantly monitored. The curator of rare books at your local university will be glad to talk with you. He or she is also desperately concerned about de-acidifying paper and is the person most likely to know who does it commercially in your district.

If you do find one of these specialists, my best advice is that you plead for an apprenticeship. I know this happens with book-binders. Toronto is the home of some of the world's most outstanding book-binders, and if one of them ever consented to allow you to stand at his elbow for two years, keeping very quiet and handing him his paste brush when asked, it would be a boon beyond price. It has been known to happen.

*   *   *   *

For those intrigued by the idea of putting together a valuable collection of books for mere pennies, the hottest field is undoubtedly paperbacks. If you know what you are looking for, you can find them for a nickel apiece among the cheapies at church bazaars and flea markets. But time is running out, and within a few years the old and the rare will have been recognized and snatched out of circulation.

Paperbacks have a history of more than 100 years, but the modern age begins just before World War II when Penguin in England and Pocket Books in the United

States introduced the format as we know it today. As with all books, the most collectible are first editions in mint condition. In this instance, "first edition" probably means first paperback edition. As time went on, paperback publishers published more and more originals, and these are that much more attractive. Sets are always interesting. A complete set of all Agatha Christie's mysteries in first paperback editions would take a lot of tracking down. First paperback editions of books which went through many subsequent editions are also worth collecting: *Catch 22*, for example, or *Catcher in the Rye.* First editions which never made it to a second are not interesting at all.

Many of the most collectible and expensive paperbacks are in the science fiction and fantasy categories. Few first paperback editions of *Lovecrafts* trade for as little as $10, and the price is going up all the time. The golden age classics are all treasured.

The best advice I can give to novice paperback collectors is to decide on two or three areas of specialty and forget the rest: *Mad Magazine* books, for example, Pelican originals, or any Canadian firsts.

BOOKPLATES

An interesting backwater just off the mainstream of book collecting is the collecting of bookplates. These are the labels gummed into the front of some books, proclaiming them to be the property of such and such a person. You can buy them new in stationery stores, and they usually have a nice picture of owls or galleons or what-have-you.

They have also been around for a long time in very large numbers, and make an interesting collectible for the sake of the design, the designer (some very good artists have done bookplates), but above all for the name or signature of a distinguished earlier owner.

I heard of one person who inherited a collection of 2,000 bookplates, some of them dating back to the 17th century and including those of such eminent men as Wilberforce, the great emancipator, Palmerston, a British Prime

Minister, and the admirals Rodney and Hood, contemporaries of Nelson.

The authoritative body seems to be the American Society of Bookplate Collectors, who tell me that most collectors belong to at least one *ex libris* society and the members exchange among themselves. Collectors of long standing are frequently generous towards newcomers to the hobby.

I wondered about the propriety of ruining a book in order to remove the bookplate, but apparently collectors haunt used book sales and thrift stores in search of damaged and not very special books which might contain interesting bookplates. Removing a good plate from a second-rate book probably would not be considered as vandalism — after buying the book, that is. Book-binders sometimes have bookplates that have been removed when a book is rebound; these turn up in family trunks and estate sales.

Most collecting is done through correspondence. A collector may write to people famous in any field who might have a library, or to college or university librarians who might know of interesting *ex libris*. Much exchanging goes on between collectors in different countries.

PRINTS

A print is some kind of pictorial representation made by a non-photographic process such as lithography, woodcut, etching, mezzotint, engraving, etc. It is safe to assume that all popular illustrations made before 1880 are prints and that almost all of those made after 1890 are photo-reproductions.

All illustrations in all books printed before 1880 were prints and the actual numbers involved might be considerable. Hundreds of thousands of copies could be run from one woodcut.

Collectibility of prints falls under two headings: artistic merit and historical interest. Good art is always treasured regardless of age. Contemporary artists make prints and sell them for a great deal of money if they are any good. Canadian artist Ken Danby, to take just one example, sells his prints for some hundreds of dollars each. This is not because they are prints, but because they are Ken Danby's.

If you are attracted to old art prints, you will need a great deal of money and even greater knowledge of the state of the market and expected future trends. There are fashions in art, and when the stakes are high the betting on futures requires a good eye and an iron nerve.

Historical prints are another matter. Travel books a century ago were published for the enlightenment and vicarious pleasure of those who stayed home, reveling in the wonders of faraway places. The more wonderful they were, the better they were likely to sell, and a poorer incentive for accuracy on the part of the writer is hard to imagine. A good travel book needs illustrations. Drawings made on the spot, recording for posterity what things looked like then, translated into engravings and used to illustrate books or sold separately to be framed are inevitably valuable. In those pre-camera days, the work of any reasonably accurate observer and draftsman was at a premium. Sketches of Canadian towns as they looked a century or more ago are treasures forever. If they are also of artistic merit, so much the better, but they do not have to be.

To verify that a print is a print rather than a photo-reproduction, all you need is a magnifying glass. A print under magnification shows a series of irregular short lines and dashes. A photo-reproduction consists in close-up of rows and rows of perfectly even, symmetrical dots.

To assist the beginner, a short list of terms may be helpful.

Woodcut	The drawing is rendered on a block of wood, and everything is chiseled away except the lines of the drawing. These lines remain raised, and when the surface is inked and pressed onto paper, only the lines of the drawing are reproduced.
Engraving	The design or picture is incised into a metal plate with a burin, a fine V-shaped chisel. The plate is inked and wiped clean, leaving residual ink only in the grooves. When soft or damp paper is pressed onto the plate, it lifts the ink out of the grooves and a print results.
Dry Point	The same process as engraving except that the engraving tool leaves a coarse edge to the groove, which leaves a softer line when printed.
Etching	The metal plate is coated with an acid-resistant compound. The artist draws his picture onto the plate, scratching through the coating with a fine, pointed instrument. When the plate is immersed in an acid solution, the exposed lines are etched leaving the coated areas untouched. Handled with subtlety, the process can be repeated several times giving a different depth of etch to selected lines.
Mezzotint	An engraving in which the entire plate is shaded by running spurred wheels over it. The artist scrapes away those parts of the picture which are to be lighter in colour.
Aquatint	A chemical process often used to achieve wash effects on etchings. To shade certain areas of an image, the artist dusts the plate with rosin powder or asphalt grain. The plate is then placed in an acid bath.
Coloured Intaglio Prints	These are usually more expensive than monochromatic examples, but they should be approached with caution. Colours would and are sometimes applied to a print after it has been printed and not necessarily by skilled workers. Whether or not the colours match what the artist had in mind is often open to question.

Lithograph Lithography has been popular among artists since its invention in 1798, because they can draw directly onto the printing stone, or zinc or aluminum plate. The drawing is done with a grease crayon or a greasy ink. The stone is stabilized with an acid solution, dampened with water and inked with a greasy ink. The ink adheres to the drawn areas but is repelled by the dampened areas. In the printing press, the ink is transferred from the stone to the paper under great pressure. Multicoloured lithographs are made by drawing images on several stones, one for each colour.

*　　*　　*　　*

An article written by William Hegeman and distributed by Toronto print dealer, Ashcroft Munro, ought to be compulsory reading for anyone with an itch to make a killing in the arts:

> Investing in prints is like investing in anything else. It takes work. Most people do not buy a company's stock without at least consulting a broker, checking whatever financial data is available and evaluating the company's potential for growth. Successful art investing calls for the same research and the same attention to detail.
>
> That means buying a few books on prints and their history so you know the difference between a lithograph and a serigraph. It also means taking the time to visit galleries and museums. Museum print shops, for instance, provide opportunities to study prints in detail, to get first-hand exposure to the difference between an etching and an engraving, or what the paper looks like on a genuine 15th century woodcut. Curators usually include descriptive material that can be tremendously useful in learning about prints. The curator is useful also as a source of recommendation as to who the good dealers in your district are. They can usually be relied on to know who is reputable and who is not. The best dealers are the real experts in the art world and have a very precise knowledge of prices. Most are unfailingly helpful in answering questions about the works in their galleries.

*　　*　　*　　*

One of the greatest names in collectible prints is George Baxter. He was born in England in 1806. As a young man he worked as a book illustrator and apprenticed as a wood engraver. He is famous less as an artist than as a pioneer in the earliest techniques of colour printing; Baxter developed a process combining wood and metal blocks that he patented in 1835.

Baxter's prints are valued today for their meticulous craftsmanship. Modern methods of colour printing employ a process known as colour separation, whereby separate printing runs in each of the primary colours plus black overlay one another to give every conceivable variation in the spectrum. Baxter's method required the hand-engraving of steel plates for every colour in the picture, something unheard of in his day. It was not unusual for him to use twenty different plates for a single picture, and rarely fewer than ten. The problems of registration, that is the precise imposition of one identical line exactly over another, twenty times over, can be imagined.

Recognition came quickly. In 1841, he attracted much attention with his remarkable "Coronation of Queen Victoria." Measuring 21 by 18 inches, the prints featured more than 200 members of the British aristocracy, each one clearly recognizable in glorious technicolour.

At the Great Exhibition of 1851 more than half a million of his prints were sold, an incredible volume of production considering the painstakingly slow methods. Seven companies are known to have produced Baxter prints under license.

Baxter was in constant financial difficulties because of high production costs. It was not until his patent expired that his process became available to others, who cheerfully reduced the number of colour plates to cut costs, while still offering them as "Baxter" prints. His own works are always mounted on creamy paper. The subjects are always "refined"; Baxter did not aspire to the sensationalism of American printmakers Currier & Ives. Colour registration is never anything but perfect, and details of flowers, jewelry or furniture always finely wrought. He retired in 1860 by which time colour lithography was making his process obsolete.

ANTIQUE MAPS

Maps are beautiful, of great historical interest and come in the most limited of editions. Maps are expensive, but prices can do nothing but grow and grow.

Who can walk past an old map without stopping to take a good look at it? Early maps were copper-plate engravings, hand-coloured in bright vegetable dyes. A price tag of $1,000 is unremarkable. The value is enhanced by the fact that early map-making was an art form, and the great cartographers of the 17th century, John Speed, Jan Janszoon and Willem Blaeu, were all famous for their beautiful and ornate work.

Here in Terra Nova or New France or Francisca or Baccalearum, an early name for Canada meaning Land of the Codfish, early maps showed us as a group of islands just off the Asian mainland. Then came Abraham Ortelius' maps showing the St. Lawrence as far inland as Hochelaga (Montreal), but he was blissfully unaware of the Great Lakes. They appeared on early Canadian maps one at a time, and it was not until the end of the 17th century that all five were recorded.

The phases of discovery in Canada are laid out on early maps. There was no West Coast before the end of the 18th century, and no northern coast until the mid-19th. Imagination ran high with early map-makers; according to them there was a great western sea covering most of what is now British Columbia and Alberta and a network of non-existent rivers all over Saskatchewan and Manitoba along which one could sail all the way from Hudson Bay to the Pacific.

Early map-makers were artists, and what is an artist without imagination? Maps made to accompany the wonderful tall tales of travel, which were the best sellers of their day, tend to reflect the tales rather than the actual topography. The rivers of Saskatchewan and the great inland sea of British Columbia all originated from a voyage attributed to an Italian Admiral DeFonte around 1750. The map-makers loved it.

There is no easy way to get into map collecting. There are no nice, cheap, little old maps for the beginner. According to Neil Sneyd of the Map Room in Toronto, few maps printed in the last 150 years are worth collecting, and only the most modest of maps older than that can be bought for as little as $100.

I challenged Mr. Sneyd with the accusation that this was a rich man's hobby, and he countered with the argument that good maps trade for sums comparable with fine art prints, which in fact is what they are. The important difference, he said, is that maps made by the early explorers and their cartographers will always be unique. For all we know there may be painters living today whose works, a couple of hundred years from now, may be more highly thought of than Rembrandt or Titian. Something similar is true for every other category of collectible — furniture, glass, ceramics, silverware — for all we know the great age is still to come. Not so with maps. Only once in the history of the planet could there be a great age of map-making and that is now at least 150 years behind us. In that case, argues Neil Sneyd with much cogency, what better investment could there be? I have yet to think of a rebuttal.

Since there is no way you are going to stumble on fine old maps at a flea market or church bazaar, I will mention a couple of dealers.

The Map Room
18 Birch Avenue,
Toronto, Ontario
M4V 1C8

Antique Map & Print Gallery
2860 West 4th Avenue,
Vancouver, British Columbia
V6K 1R2

Swift coffee mill, circa 1900.

7 Collectibles

It is difficult to come to grips with a subject like collectibles without dropping things into artificial categories where in practice there are no categories. We tend to think of collectibles, antiques, folk art, crafts and fine art as though they are something different, but in fact it would be hard to find any item mentioned in these pages which does not rightfully belong under at least two, and more often three, of these headings.

The only indisputable definition of a collectible is "anything anyone wants to collect," and that embraces just about everything from matchbox tops to ancient Greek statues. In common usage the word tends to refer to articles which were manufactured with no thought of future collectibility; things which were mass-produced, used briefly and discarded in almost equally massive quantities. What is left is a tiny percentage of the original output but still substantial enough to attract a body of collectors.

There is no time factor. Some fruit jars are more than 100 years old but are thought of as collectibles rather than antiques. Others, more recent, like 45 rpm rock and roll records, have a substantial body of enthusiasts. Still others, such as Royal Wedding commemoratives and Olympic coins, are definitely made to be collected, while such items as Depression glass and Occupied Japan ceramics are categorized elsewhere. The following is no more than a tiny representative selection.

TOKENS

There are signs that token collecting is one of our fastest growing hobbies. It is an enormous subject, which is appealing to an even larger number of people. The use of tokens as a medium of exchange covers a long period of time in Canadian history. From the early bank and merchant's token of the colonies to the present-day municipal fund-raising issues, collectors have a wide and varied field from which to choose.

The token collector can specialize in any one of a large number of categories: early railway tokens, general merchants' due bills, tradesmen's cards, bar checks, dairy and bakery tokens, transportation and car wash tokens, communion tokens and the currently popular municipal issues, or medallions, tokens and scrip.

No aspect of Canadian numismatics portrays the history of this country better than its tokens. Good examples are the early tokens of the companies engaged in the fur trade such as The Hudson's Bay Company and others.

The subject is rich in folklore. For example, the Chilliwack Chamber of Commerce issued a trade dollar in 1978 to celebrate the First International Camel Race. The race never took place because the camels failed to comply with health standards and the coin shows a camel fleeing from federal health officials. I don't know if the Chilliwack Chamber of Commerce has any left, but at $1 each, they are a bargain.

My crystal ball informs me that one of the truly great collectibles of the future is precisely this kind of commemorative dollar, issued in celebration of special events in all parts of Canada. They are usually legal tender locally for about a month, but then what happens to them? One of these days they are going to be worth a great deal of money.

COUNTRY STORE COLLECTIBLES

The term "country store collectable" is not terribly accurate. Actually we mean "general store" because, of course, the old city stores had the same attractive stuff. The connotation of a country store, however, with its hint of nostalgia, variety and warmth, conveys the attraction of this kind of collecting. It includes advertising — signs, posters, trade cards and all sorts of give-away items which range from stuffed dolls to small furniture, all imprinted with a commercial message. It also includes store fixtures like coffee mills, dispensers, large bins, mirrors and so on . . . anything, in fact that is pleasant to look at, to display or to wonder about and that recalls an older, less sophisticated time.

Country Store Collectables, Bill and Pauline Hogan

There is something beguiling about country store collectibles, those colourful old cans, trays, metal signs and thermometers of long ago. They pluck at everyone's nostalgic chords, including collectors far too young to remember them. The market has been given a tremendous boost by some of the fast food people, like Mother's Pizza, who decorate their premises with memorabilia of the days before pizza was invented, encouraging new collectors while creating shortages and the kind of inflation rate that only a collector would love.

The old cans, coffee mills and tin signs that decorate your local hamburger joint will have been picked up from many sources. Their authenticity is not in question but the majority will be American in origin and therefore of little interest to Canadian collectors. Canadian cans are much rarer and therefore more challenging.

Old tobacco tins head the list of desirability. Gramps will be chagrined to learn that those old tin pouches of Taxi Crimp Cut, which he used to smoke during World War I, are now trading at more than $700 each. The Gold Dust pouch is labeled "Worth Its Weight in Gold," and since it too now trades for around $650, empty, that would be about right. King Edward Crimp Cut and one of the Forest and Stream pouches at $125 and $150 respectively are among the lesser items.

Tobacco and cigarette boxes bear more democratic price tags. Mooney's at $30,

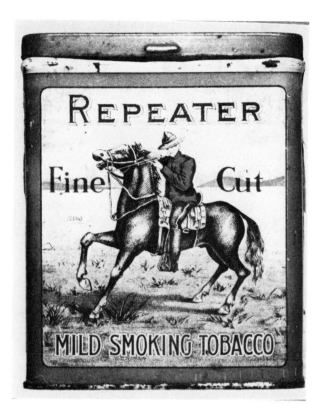

Repeater Smoking Tobacco tin, circa 1910.

Harrison Cady, who illustrated this can, was also the illustrator of Thornton Burgess's Peter Rabbit *books.*

Capitol Ceylon Blend Tea tin.

Clubb's Dollar Mixture at $8, and Horseshoe at $5 give some idea of the price range. I paid 50¢ for a Horseshoe tin five years ago, a profit of 1,000 percent, which I shall doubtless spend on riotous living.

Tobacco tins are followed by peanut butter pails, coffee cans, tea tins, starch containers, candy pails, ointment and phonograph needle tins, signs, trays and dispensers in approximate order of popularity, though not necessarily in price. Diamond Dye Dispenser trades for $400; Dr. Daniel's Veterinary Medicine Cabinet for $350 and Clark & Co.'s Anchor Spool Cotton cabinet for $175.

Please remember these are 1980 prices and already out of date!

POSTCARDS

Back in 1974 I paid $75 to an American collector for 500 pre-World War I postcards depicting Canadian street scenes. I sold them immediately for $250. It was a very satisfactory rate of profit for that time, but today those same cards could hardly be worth less than $1,500.

There is little doubt that postcard collecting is one of our fastest growing hobbies and one with a very bright future. Collector clubs are springing up, and we have seen the beginnings of shows and swap-meets devoted exclusively to postcards.

Enthusiasts call themselves "deltiologists," a word that dates back to 1930 when an American collector coined the term which allegedly has Greek roots. The great years of the postcard were 1900 to 1914. Not only were they widely used in an age when mail was fast and cheap and there were no telephones, but they were also considered collectible even then. "Here is another card for your collection" is a fairly common message still to be read in the faded ink of the period. Travellers sent postcards to their friends and relatives, and the pictures of the places they visited were always the most popular.

The numbers involved are enormous. The J.V. Valentine Company, one of the early postcard publishers, turned out one to two tons of postcards every working day. They were located in Dundee, Scotland, where they printed over 20,000 Canadian scenes. Other suppliers were Raphael Tuck of England and George Stewart of Edinburgh. One of the major manufacturers in Canada was Warwick Bros. & Rutter of Toronto. New Brunswick and Nova Scotia were serviced by the Valentine & Sons Publishing Company, presumably a subsidiary of the Dundee firm. Nova Scotia also had W.G. MacFarlane of Toronto and E.S. Helier of Halifax. E.H. Davis & Company did pictures of Yarmouth. Novelty Mfg. & Art Co. of Montreal and Carter & Co. supplied Prince Edward Island, while British Columbia abounded in postcard manufacturers too numerous to list.

Continuous new issues of postcards kept the hobby up to date and provided a unique record of the changing facade of every Canadian town.

For a collector to try to acquire every pre-World War I card showing scenes of a city the size of Toronto would be an impossible task. Many thousands of cards would be involved. As with most mass collectibles, the field must be narrowed to make it manageable — churches, banks, bridges, post offices and railway stations are just a few of the possible categories, and even these run to very large numbers.

Collectible postcards are by no means limited to street scenes. One collector has a fancy for pictures of dog carts. Most of us have never seen a dog cart; even fewer of us have ever seen a postcard of a dog cart. He has over 140 of them — all different. One American

A 1909 Toronto postcard.

This postcard from the early 1900s was published by Stephen J. Thompson, Publisher, Vancouver, British Columbia.

Arrival of Jacques Cartier at Quebec.1535

Many companies used the postcard as an advertising vehicle.

A postcard from the days of elegant train travel.

magazine speaks of more than 8,000 postcards, all related in some way to President Lincoln. No subject, it seems, was missed by those enterprising old-time postcard designers.

Beyond subject matter, there are other specialities such as embossed cards, hand-painted cards and those rare and beautiful cards made by French women during World War I and sold to Canadian soldiers who sent them home.

There are greeting cards, Halloween, Christmas, New Year's and Valentine's Day, very colourful, charming, and enormously popular with today's collectors.

We are well past the Golden Age of Canadian postcard collecting. Even though many thousands of them are still languishing in forgotten trunks in forgotten attics, when at last they do see the light of day they will not be offered for 15¢. Most of the market as we know it is now securely in the hands of dealers and collectors, and with more and more people discovering the fascination of deltiology, supply and demand can only result in ever upward price trends.

MILITARY COLLECTIBLES

Military collectibles is one of those subjects that can hardly be addressed at all other than through one of its many categories. From cap badges to army tanks, the artifacts of war are, from the collector's point of view, both numerous and fascinating. History itself is barely distinguishable from military history, and it is possible to focus on any battle, let alone any war, as fully collectible in its own right. Moreover, because Canada is a mosaic of many cultures, an immigrant may well choose the military history of his own country of origin.

Canada, the least bellicose of nations, has a rich military history of its own, and since the planting of a flag rarely fails to elicit troop movements, those who pursue military badges have a virtually endless task in front of them if their objective is no more than one badge from every regiment that ever served in this country.

Badges do not stay the same forever; new theatres of service, new honours or royal appointments all contribute to the evolution of a military badge. Regiments are disbanded or amalgamated with others, and the collector must delve into a great deal of regimental history if his collection is to be in any way meaningful.

Then there are the medals, both those that, as we used to say, "came round with the rations," and were issued to everyone just for being there, and medals of merit and courage all the way up to the coveted Victoria Cross. A medal for merit without the story that goes with it is poor stuff indeed if it becomes collectible for itself rather than serving to commemorate the bravery of its recipient. It is the task and the pleasure of the dedicated medal collector to search the records for the history of the man. The summer 1981 issue of CSMMI, the official journal of the Canadian Society of Military Medals and Insignia, records one such piece of research by James J. Grosberg, who resurrected a long dead soldier of the Boer War whose only memorial is a fairly commonplace medal:

> Arthur Francis Hoyland, 20 years, 3 months, stove grate worker. 5'11," 126 pounds, blue-eyed and Church of England. Signed the oath on Jan. 3, 1900 at Sheffield, England.
>
> His medical certificate states that "He can see at the required distance with either eye, his hearing and lungs are healthy, he has free use of his joints and limbs, and he declares that he is not subject to fits." On the 8th of January he was approved by a Colonel whose signature is illegible. His total pension from engagement to death was calculated at 185 days, all entries being verified by Major H. Richards.
>
> He is listed as having been killed at Bethlehem, South Africa, on July 6, 1900.

Thus history comes alive.

Military memorabilia is by no means limited to badges and medals, although these are appealing by reason of the numbers still available. Firearms are invariably popular; swords, daggers and similar articles of mayhem have their adherents; drums, regimental horse brasses, helmets, indeed complete uniforms, are eagerly sought by enthusiasts; while for the specialists there are military antiquities going all the way back to suits of armour and battle axes.

Military paper, too, is highly collectible; regimental histories, service manuals, citations,

A shako of the Third Incorporated Militia, 1840-1842.

A Royal Canadian Mounted Police officer's helmet, circa 1920.

rolls of honour, programmes of ceremonial troopings of the colour on great occasions are all grist for the mill. Private diaries of serving soldiers are of the highest military significance.

This brief outline serves only as an introduction to a vast subject. I have been speaking of military collectibles as if only the army was of interest. The navy and air force are obviously rich in history and very collectible. The same is true of such allied services as the coastguard and the R.C.M.P.

Another important factor is that there are still rich treasures to be discovered. Military memorabilia, especially mementos of those who never came back, tend to survive, and even if they are neglected, there is a proper reluctance to throw them out.

Beware the pickers who will offer to take "worthless" old medals off your hands for the price of the silver; they are worth far more than that. Best idea is to check with one of the military collector societies listed in the back of the book, or a specialist dealer.

PHONOGRAPH RECORDS

A friend of mine who sells at our local flea market thought he was on to a good thing a year or two back when he started buying quantities of old 78 records from people's attics for 10¢ each and selling them for 50¢ each — a handsome 500 percent markup. Record collectors made a beeline for his table, and sales were brisk. After three months, he took his entire stock down to the dump and went out of the record business. How come? Sales were brisk, but he was selling far fewer than one in five of those he bought. He was therefore losing money. Moreover, the number of unsold records was piling up at an alarming rate. Before he dumped them he tried to unload the lot, over 1,000 records, onto other dealers; for 5¢ each, 2¢, and finally $10 for the lot. There were no takers.

The moral of the story is that there are huge numbers of old 78s to be had, but very, very few of them are worth anything at all. The mistake made by those who are hoping to sell their old records is to assume that collectors are in search of round black things with labels in the middle. They are not, not unless the label is an extremely rare one. They are music lovers, and like all of today's music lovers reared on stereophonic perfection, they are only interested in old records that are virtually brand-new. The price guides list something like Bing Crosby's pre-1934 recording on Brunswick of "Love in Bloom" at $7.50. This may not seem like an exciting price to the non-collector but in fact marks it a very desirable record. But that $7.50 will be paid only for a disc that has never been out of its jacket. A moment's thought will confirm that this makes it a rare object indeed. Who would buy it not to play it? Who would play it only once or twice considering it was one of the "tops of the pops" in its day? If it had not been a hit, it would not now be collectible.

Thus the problem. There is nothing rare about old 78s, there are still literally millions of them around, but to command any price at all they have to be in pristine condition.

Another myth is that the older they are, the better. Not so. As a period, the most collectible is certainly the 1930s. The Depression nearly destroyed the record business, and the rise in popularity of radio almost made it redundant. Sales were small and piracy was worse. Piracy consisted of the re-recording by dubious companies of existing records by popular groups. In other areas of collecting, these would be rejected as reproductions, which is exactly what they are. Record collectors, however, treasure them.

Most collectible records trade in the $2 to $5 bracket. A positive galaxy of famous names are dismissed as N.M.P. meaning Negligible Market Potential. These include such stars as Eddy Duchin, Deanna Durbin, Wayne King, Dorothy Lamour, Carmen Miranda, Vaughn Monroe, Dick Powell, Jo Stafford and Frank Sinatra. Early jazz is good. "Satchmo" Louis Armstrong ranges from $1.50 ("Jeepers Creepers") to $35 ("Gut Bucket Blues"). Early Duke Ellingtons, Fletcher Hendersons, Earl Hines and the New Orleans Rhythm Kings all list in the $25 to $50 bracket.

Country and Western is very collectible. There are rumours of $100 paid for a mint Jimmy Rogers. We are talking about pre-war, pre-Nashville C. & W. scraped out on mountain dulcimers and banjos, weird amalgams of Elizabethan folk music and African blues. The themes were love and pain, hardship and everlastingly travelling on. The luckiest break for country singers then was when someone paid them a stunning $50 to make a record. Rarely more. Few of them ever made a second record. That is why old C. & W. music stands somewhere near the top of the collectible tree and is likely to remain there.

A typical patriotic song from World War 1.

Pre-World War 1 advertising ditty.

One of the many hit songs of the Dumbells.

SHEET MUSIC

There are several price guides to sheet music published in the United States, one sure indication that it is a popular collectible — as it should be. Music is the greatest of all pop arts, and there is nothing as nostalgic as the hit tunes of our teen years. We remember the words all our lives.

Collectors tend to select their own pet speciality, and the following categories will give some idea of the many possibilities: songs by Irving Berlin, songs from Fred Astaire/Ginger Rogers films, songs of Al Jolson, songs of the First or Second World War, songs from Broadway shows, songs of any particular year and, maybe the most popular category of all, song sheets with interesting or artistic covers. The most popular and pricey of American song sheets are those by E.T. Paull. Their stunning lithographed covers printed by A. Hoen of Richmond, Virginia are certainly worth framing. There are collectors of what are still known as "coon" songs, early jazz and blues, ragtime and sheet music bearing pictures of movie stars.

Music published before 1885 is always worth looking at for the picture on the cover.

Those were pre-photo-reproduction days, and all the illustrations would be steel engravings, woodcuts, etchings, lithographs or any one of the techniques known as "prints." Whether or not they are of any value in their own right is determined purely by their artistic merit.

I would assume, but with little evidence to support it, that all old Canadian sheet music is potentially valuable. I have picked up many dozen such pieces quite indiscriminately at flea markets and garage sales. Most of it consists of patriotic songs of World War I, dripping with maple leaves. There are some fairly old commercial songs, Nukol Sparks, the "Burning Love Song," for example; mined, pressed and delivered by Jules Brazil, and published by Anglo-Canadian Music Publishers in 1919. The chorus reads, "So we'll use Nukol. Yes we'll use Nukol. It hasn't got clinkers, it hasn't got slate; saves pain in your back caused by shaking the grate . . . "

Another is called "I'll Be Your Rain-beau — I'll Beam For You," compliments of the Comfort Soap Company of Toronto. On the back is a list of premiums, such as a gold-filled 14K ring set with a single stone, choice of emerald, amethyst or opal for 100 Comfort Soap wrappers and 25¢. Yet another is "The Song of the Hub," by George White, written for the Kiwanis Club of New Liskeard in honour of their hometown. "At the head of the lake was a hamlet, where a few sturdy souls settled down, and these pioneers from the southland, founded Liskeard our own little town." It also says "Copyright 1828," presumably a misprint.

The "W-R Two Step," by J.B. Glionna was commissioned by Whaley-Royce. In 1895, the company's pianos were guaranteed for seven years, but they are still going strong 85 years later.

My favourite piece is a handwritten gem called "The Dying Engineer." "He was lonely and sad, he was far from home and weary with pain he was lying; a brave engineer, he had saved his train yet he knew he would soon be dying."

These examples come from my own Canadian collection. I very much doubt if any of them are valuable — yet.

Early pull toys, circa 1880-1910.

8 Miscellaneous

This chapter is reserved for all those delightful items that are a joy to collect but don't fit into any particular category.

CANADIAN HERALDRY

Some aspects of collecting open up fascinating avenues of research that could become absorbing subjects in their own right. The collector who puts one toe into the water might easily find himself literally carried away.

A very good example of this is heraldry. At first glance, it would seem to be one of those esoteric topics interesting only to English nobility, but a moment's thought will confirm a wealth of Canadian examples. These are not limited to Canadians whose genealogies trace

The Canadian coat of arms of Sir William Alexander, who was made a Baronet of Nova Scotia in 1621.

back to the great families of Europe; they include every college, every bank, municipality and province that has its own armorial device.

Colonel A. Strome Galloway, Hon. Editor of *Heraldry in Canada*, generously contributed the following introduction to what is clearly a vast subject.

When we speak of collecting Canadian heraldry, we mean the collecting of various antiques which have a national, municipal, institutional or personal heraldic device on them indicating original ownership. A prime example is found in the collecting of armorial bookplates, those paper squares bearing shields or crests which armigerous organizations or persons paste inside the covers of their books to indicate ownership. Next we think of silver with engraved armorial devices — fork handles, porringers, teapots and so on. Armorial porcelain with painted arms, or crystal with etched arms are also popular collector's items. Less likely to be collected are items of furniture with carved or painted heraldic embellishments, or stained glass windows and marble floor inlays — all of which were popular methods of displaying armigerous status in the days when "people of quality" put considerable store in the prestige of being an armiger.

Of course it may take considerable research to determine whether the arms, crests or full heraldic achievements are genuine or bogus. The newly-rich industrialist and wealthy social-climber of the 19th century was not above "adopting" ("usurping" would be a better word) the armorial entitlements of others to increase his own social prestige. Frequently, this was on the mistaken idea that a surname and a coat-of-arms, or crest, were one and the same. This was, and is, nonsense. Unfortunately, this false belief was aided and abetted by stationers, silversmiths and other such merchants in Great Britain as well as Canada, and as a result, many Canadian families blossomed forth with crested writing paper and signet rings, armorial seals, watches, trays and salvers in the mistaken belief that because their family names, shall we say, were Russell, Stanley or Howard, they were entitled to the armorial devices of the Lords Amptill, the Earls of Derby or the Dukes of Norfolk, who by mere coincidence also bore these surnames.

The antique collector, therefore, must do a certain amount of detective work before getting excited over an armorial find on some set of silver candlesticks or an armorial embroidered firescreen, or any other heraldically embellished antique.

It must be remembered that no shield of arms, crest or complete armorial achievement has any connection whatsoever with a surname *per se*. Over the centuries, grants of arms were made by sovereigns to eminent subjects on petition and on payment of fees. This is still the procedure and is done through the Officers of Arms of the Crown. Arms then descend in the direct male line, and entitlement should be made up by lawful means each succeeding generation.

Antique collectors who come upon apparently desirable items bearing heraldic devices should ensure that such devices are genuine, that they do indeed identify the original ownership they purport to identify, or if they are usurped arms, that such is duly noted. The best way to ensure that one is not misled by mere heraldic beauty is to consult an expert. The Heraldic Society of Canada is a recommended consultant if this sort of assistance is required.

You do not have to be "armigerous" to join the Heraldry Society of Canada. Regular membership is $25 annually, and members receive their colourful quarterly magazine. The main purpose of this society is to inform Canadians of correct heraldic practices through articles, lectures and exhibitions. It maintains a Roll of Arms of members and acts as a clearing-house for legitimate enquiries on heraldry from municipalities, institutions, corporations and individuals, providing them with information on correct heraldic practices. The society's address is 125 Lakeway Drive, Ottawa, Ontario K1L 5A9.

FRAKTUR

The art of *Fraktur* originated in the German settlements of Continental Europe and Russia. It reached Canada in two waves: the first as a tradition practised by Pennsylvania-German settlers who migrated north in the early 19th century and settled in Ontario's Niagara region, in Vaughan and Markham townships just north of Toronto and in Waterloo County; the second wave was a result of the settlers of German origin who arrived in the Canadian West from Russia during the latter portion of the century.

This charming 1875 drawing is by Fraktur *artist, Anna Weber.*

Fraktur is a form of ornamental hand-lettering and drawing used on baptismal records, marriage certificates and family documents of all kinds. It is characterized by gothic calligraphy, colourful hearts, tulips, birds, stylized trees and floral motifs of many kinds. Today, these lettered and decorated documents are eminently collectible items, including those from Manitoba and Saskatchewan that have only recently been recognized for what they are.

Early practitioners of *Fraktur* were occasionally itinerant folk artists who traveled the countryside offering their services from door to door in Germanic settlements of Pennsylvania, Maryland, Virginia, Ohio and Ontario. Others, like Ontario's Anna Weber, were shut-ins whose health might prevent outdoor movement but whose artistic abilities were not impaired.

The Pennsylvania-German community established in Lincoln County, on the shores of Lake Ontario, seems to be the earliest centre in which Canadian *Fraktur* was practised. These pioneers sent out satellite groups to

A splendid example of Ontario Fraktur.

settle in the Welland area and parts of
Haldimand-Norfolk. The dominant form then,
around the turn of the 18th century, was the
Vorschrift, an illustrated book, specimen
lettered by a teacher to be copied by pupils.

One unnamed *Fraktur* artist seems to have
traveled from family to family across southern
Ontario executing hand-lettered birth records
and family trees. From the trail of examples he
left, it appears that his swing through Ontario
must have occurred during the 1800-1810
period.

Like the invalid Anna Weber, Christian L.
Hoover took up the art as a kind of
occupational therapy after a bout of fever left
him bed-ridden. He kept himself busy
producing birth records for his brothers,
sisters and other relatives. All known examples
from his hand date from 1854 and 1855.

With the establishment of Mennonite
settlements in Waterloo County, *Fraktur* enters
a period of folk art at its very best. Now the

important names begin to emerge. There was
Abraham Latschaw, better known as a great
cabinetmaker. His double bookplate/
genealogy for the Bible of Bishop Benjamin
Eby, spiritual leader of Mennonites in
Waterloo County, is probably the masterpiece
of Ontario *Fraktur*. The calligraphy is superb
and all is harmoniously blended with tulips,
birds, angels and other folk motifs. He seems
to have practised the art for no more than a
single year, and one has to wonder what might
have resulted if only he had continued. Isaac Z.
Hunsicker was a more prolific artist who left a
fairly substantial body of works in the form of
bookplates and family registers. Anna Weber
was well into her fifties before she seriously
took up *Fraktur* and she went on to devote the
next twenty years to the art. In kindness to
future collectors, she signed and dated her
work, often adding the name of the recipient.
A fourth Waterloo County artist was Joseph
D. Bauman who made drawings, family
registers and decorated Adam and Eve
broadsides. With his death in 1899 the great

age of Waterloo *Fraktur* comes to an end.

Beyond the examples of great *Fraktur* left by those mentioned above, there remain numerous anonymous pieces and those done by school children, many of which employ religious symbols. *Fraktur* right now is little more than a word to frighten Scrabble opponents, but I suspect we are going to hear a great deal more about it. This is folk art at its best and all predictions for antique futures suggest that 19th century folk art is about to go through the roof.

APOSTLE SPOONS

Apostle spoons date back to pre-Elizabethan times. By the late 15th century they were in general use and they remained that way until Oliver Cromwell and the Puritans condemned them as religious images. They stayed out of favour until the mid-19th century, when there was a great and continuing revival of interest.

Early Apostle spoons had hexagonal stems, fig-shaped bowls and very often the head of the figure wore a halo. They rarely turn up at country auctions because by now any that have survived are in museums or change hands between private collectors for huge sums.

Ancient tradition has given each Apostle a symbol related in some way to the manner in which he died. All were martyred, save for St. John, who is said to have lived to be a hundred.

Here are the Apostles and their emblems:
St. Peter — the key
St. Andrew — the x-shaped cross
St. James the Greater — the sword
St. John — the cup of sorrow
St. Thomas — a spear
St. James the Less — a dye-maker's paddle
St. Philip — a staff with a cross at the end
St. Bartholomew — a flaying knife
St. Matthew — a money bag
St. Matthias — an axe
St. Simon the Zealot — a long saw
St. Jude — a club or fish
That makes 12. Judas Iscariot was usually replaced by St. Matthias. Some sets were also accompanied by a Master spoon in which Christ was portrayed holding the Orb and the Cross in his left hand with his right hand raised

in benediction. These emblems are not exclusive to spoons and were used in all early religious art. They were standard symbols except in the case of St. Matthias, St. Thomas and St. Jude, for whom there are German and Italian variations.

TOOLS

Perhaps the last group of genuine antiques to emerge from Canada's Golden Age as authentic collectibles are 19th century hand tools. Prices are going up in leaps and bounds yet they are still to be found in quantities in flea markets. Doubtless far larger numbers lurk in barns all over the country.

Collector interest in old hand tools is a phenomenon of the last year or two, but already in Toronto we have seen the first show devoted more or less exclusively to them, and at least one dealer is specializing in them.

The field is vast, just how vast is still unknown. What we are talking about here are the last remnants of the pre-industrial age, when, it must be remembered, everything still had to be done — somehow — one way or another. Houses were built, ships were built, furniture was made, as well as carriages, barrels and wrought-iron articles of all kinds. Butchers, bakers and candlestick-makers all needed their own specialized tools as did dentists, surgeons and barbers. Woodsmen's

A typical display of tools at a tool show.

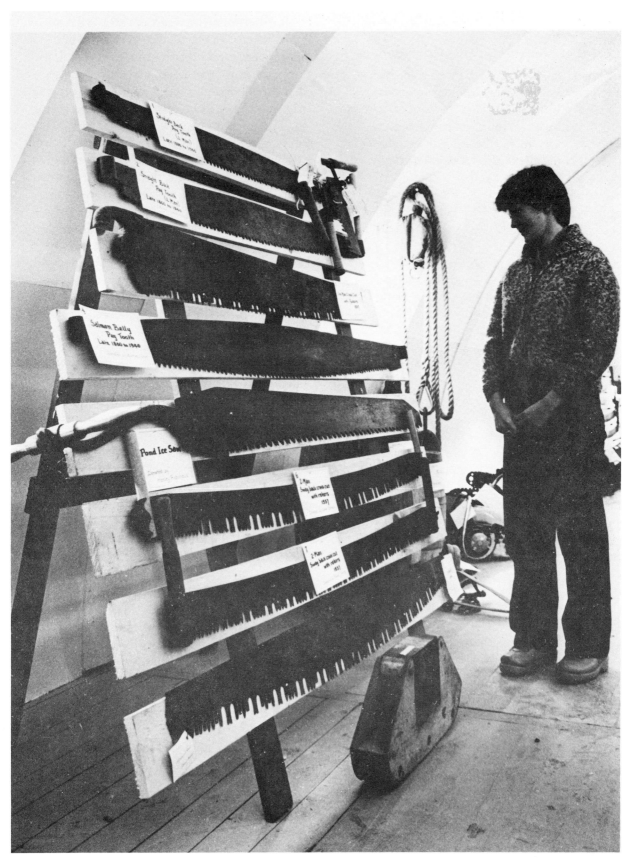

A museum exhibit of saws for various purposes.

tools are a complete collectible in their own right, as are those of the blacksmith and the farmer.

In what is still the infancy of a new collectible, people are eclectic in their pickings, but specialization is inevitable. There are hundreds of different kinds of axes, hundreds of different planes, hundreds of chisels, cooper's tools, farrier's tools and carriage-maker's tools all waiting to be properly identified and categorized.

Pioneer villages are great places to see and get information about 19th century hand tools, and museums all over the country, especially those dealing with particular trades such as ship-building, mining or logging, are excellent sources of information. Meanwhile, acquire all tools wherever you find them; they make a handsome display and are still generally underpriced. And is anyone willing to guarantee that we are not going to need them again?

TREEN

I have argued that there is no such word, but it appears that Saxons were using it a thousand years ago when it meant "wooden." It still does. If, as I believe, we are about to witness a surge of enthusiasm for folk art, treen will serve as a perfect illustration of the problems which confront both collectors and those writing for them.

Maple sugar mould, 19th century.

After "what's it worth," the two questions that collectors most often ask are "who made it and when." As far as treen is concerned, answers are rarely forthcoming. "Treen" does not just mean "made from wood" but also "handmade from wood," and the Saxon origins indicate how long this has been going on. There are, to be sure, many factory-made kitchen items such as rolling pins and potato mashers, but the treen enthusiast is unlikely to wax eloquent about anything that came from a lathe. We are talking, therefore, about things that were whittled, carved or scooped by untold numbers of people whose names were never recorded, all the way back to the beginnings of recorded history. Designs are almost universal. Wooden bowls made in Canada, Central America, Africa, India, Polynesia or Japan are distinguishable only by the wood from which they were made and local distinctions of decoration.

What then is the collector looking for? How can an early 19th century Canadian butter bowl be distinguished from one imported from Mexico within the last 12 months?

My own impression is that it is far from easy to fake an authentic-looking butter bowl. You only have to see examples of the real thing — and this applies to all treen — to know with reasonable certainty that here is something worn smooth by thousands of handlings in the same way that the foot of a marble saint may be worn smooth by the touch of thousands of worshippers. Finally the collector has to rely on her or his sensitivity to the human touch.

There are few native trees which have not been used by old-time domestic whittlers and few household implements that were not at one time made of wood. It was the most readily available material and could be worked with the most rudimentary of skills.

On the other hand, the hundreds of thousands of indifferently made treen pieces have long since gone to kindling, and the law of the survival of the fittest determines what remains with us. Generally speaking, what survives is what was worthy to survive.

Certainly, from the collector's point of view, few artifacts retain such charm or conjure up our pioneer past so vividly.

Pequegnat schoolhouse clock.

CLOCKS

Canada came late to industrial clock-making. The short-lived Hamilton Clock Company, later named Canada Clocks, lasting from 1877 to 1886, was preceded only by individual clock and watch-makers, like Twiss of Montreal. The early part of the 19th century was dominated by the superb craft factories of Connecticut, names such as Eli Terry, Chauncey Jerome, Silas Hoadey and Seth Thomas, whose clocks were flooding the world's markets.

A.S. Whiting, who came to Canada in the 1840s, would bring 100 clocks from a factory in New England by boat to Port Hope. There he would buy a team of horses and a spring wagon and with the clocks on board, start on a selling tour of the surrounding district. Arriving at a farmhouse, he would set up a clock in the kitchen. Having partaken of the meal which was invariably offered, or remained for the night, he would depart leaving the clock which he said would be collected some weeks later on his return trip. But so convenient did the farmers find this new fangled contraption that he very seldom had to take the clock back. In those early days a traveller was never asked to pay for a meal or lodging at a farmhouse. The budget of news he brought was considered fair payment.

Edmund Burrows, *Canadian Clocks and Clockmakers*

Early Canadian clocks whose makers can be identified are well worth collecting. This piece was made and signed by Nelson Walker, Montreal, Quebec, in the early 19th century.

It was not until the end of the great clock-making era that Canada came into its own in the person of Arthur Pequegnat (pronounced Peginaw), who came to Kitchener, Ontario, in 1874 when it was still known as Berlin and set up a jewelry store. He was an ingenious, industrious man of iron integrity who was always a little behind the times. He built a factory to make bicycles in 1897, only to have the bottom drop out of the bike trade in 1903. He then switched to clocks, which the company continued to make until 1940, oblivious to style changes which made their line ever more obsolescent.

On the other hand, Pequegnat scored on sheer workmanship. His catalogue states:

We are satisfied that if a careful comparison is made of Pequegnat clocks with competing lines, the results will prove very much to our advantage, for even a hurried inspection cannot fail to convince that in construction our movements are unexcelled while in workmanship and finish, Pequegnat clock movements are vastly superior and our clock cases are much more substantially constructed. We do not ask you to favour us with your trade simply because we are the only Canadian clock-makers but have conclusively demonstrated for so many years that we make the best clocks on the market.

Collectors today confirm that Pequegnat's claims are no more than the truth. It says a great deal about the sheer character of the man that he remained convinced that superior quality would prevail despite all the evidence that he could only fight a rearguard action against the electric clock which invaded the domestic market as early as 1915.

TEXTILES

Since I am convinced that the next significant wave of inflation to hit the antique market is going to carry folk art way up on the price scale, something needs to be said about textiles. Ruth McKendry's book *Quilts and Other Bed Coverings in the Canadian Tradition* and Mary Conroy's book *300 Years of Canadian Quilts* did much to revive interest in Canadian needlecrafts. However, my guess is that there is still research to be done in this area.

Needlecrafts are attractive because each is an example of individual craftsmanship. Such pieces could not be duplicated today for anything even close to the prices they are presently fetching on the antique market (when they appear at all). Every form — lace, crochet, tatting, etc. — is demanding, meticulous and time-consuming.

There was a time when skill with the needle was a mandatory part of a young girl's training. The "sampler," for example, was exactly what its name implies, an example of a girl's proficiency, not only with the needle but also

in spelling and numbers. Samplers are a complete study in themselves going far beyond the "Home Sweet Home" platitudes into special areas such as map samplers — elaborate, rare and marvellously valuable.

One thing it would be interesting to know is how and when these little girls did all this exquisite work. Their chores filled all the daylight hours, and surely they did not work those tiny stitches by the dubious light of the pre-kerosene age. This is a fascinating question in itself. What did people do after dark when there was no better illumination than a whale oil lamp?

Early needlework is by no means restricted to samplers. That was kid's stuff. Having gained proficiency by the age of ten, these girls were only then at the beginning of a lifetime of crocheting, embroidering, smocking, hemstitching, candlewicking, hooking rugs, making wool and silk comforters, carding, dyeing, spinning, weaving, knitting and darning for their huge families. They made the clothes they wore and all the household linen; the fact that there was any time left over for artistic flights of fancy boggles the imagination.

The history of textiles is a fascinating area, full of snippets of folklore every bit as charming as the objects themselves. An Acadian girl was not permitted to marry until she could weave a piece of cloth. Among the pioneers, a girl started her first quilt at the age of six and was expected to have thirteen of them in her dower chest when she married. The last one, the bridal quilt, bore symbols of love, fertility and longevity. It was considered bad luck to start the bridal quilt until there was a prospect of marriage, and in some parts of Canada it was bad luck for a girl to work on her own bridal quilt. Friends and neighbours made it for her. Quilting bees in New Brunswick were called "frolics."

A piece of cloth enjoyed several lives. It might start off as a man's jacket, be cut down to make coats for a succession of children and wind up in a quilt or a hooked rug. A pioneer wife could often trace the history of a piece of cloth back through sixty years.

*　　*　　*　　*

This 1883 sampler from Ontario records the birth
of its maker, Anna Martin, and her two brothers.

Whether or not textiles are safe investments for the future may depend to a large extent on how well they are stored. Under ideal conditions natural fabrics will last a very long time — the famous shroud of Turin is an example — but ideal conditions are rarely met.

Here are a few tips suggested by the National Museums of Canada, Textile Division Conservation Service of 1030 Innes Road, Ottawa, which should be consulted on all such matters.

1. Beware of excessive light. Avoid ultra-violet radiation and extremes of humidity and temperature. Colours will fade and fibres become brittle as a direct result of light intensity and ultra-violet radiation. High humidity encourages the growth of moulds, while low humidity results in dessication and embrittlement.

   It is best to use incandescent lamps of medium wattage. Do not use daylight lamps and check the ultra-violet output of whatever fluorescents you are using. It is wisest to keep textiles in the dark. They should only be exposed to light when you want to look at them.

2. Try for a maximum summer humidity of 58 percent and a minimum winter humidity of 25 percent. Avoid rapid changes in humidity. Temperature is less critical. Whatever you personally find comfortable is probably OK for textiles too.

3. Insects pose the greatest threat. Do not allow textiles to get dirty. Mothballs and other repellents are only a way of buying time; at best they only retard infestation until the fabric can be cleaned. They are only effective in closed containers or confined spaces. If infestation is severe, it may be necessary to fumigate, in which case it is advisable to check with the above-mentioned Conservation Service for safe methods.

4. When storing, remove all old newspaper wrappings to avoid acid transfer. Remove coloured tissue to prevent running dyes. Remove paddings, pins and staples.

5. Store textiles flat. Allow for the greatest amount of fibre relaxation and a minimum of abrasion. If you must fold the article, place crumpled acid-free tissue in the folds for structural support to prevent the fibres from breaking along the creases. When moving, do not re-fold along the same creases.

6. Avoid contact between fabrics and unsealed wooden or cardboard surfaces, which may be assumed to be acidic. Line the bottom and sides of boxes with acid-free paper. Choose large boxes to minimize folding.

7. Textiles should not be stacked directly on top of one another as the weight may damage the piece underneath. If pieces must be stacked, separate layers with acid-free tissue.

8. One good way of storing textiles is to roll them onto tubes which can often be obtained free of charge from carpet stores. Layer with acid-free tissue. Make sure there are no folds or creases created in the rolling process. Cover in washed muslin.

9. Check with your local museum for a source of acid-free tissue.

ART NOUVEAU, ART DECO AND KITSCH

John Mebane in *The Complete Book of Collecting Art Nouveau* describes Art Nouveau as one of the shortest-lived art movements of modern times. It flourished briefly around the end of the century and represents art's last gasp before surrendering to the machine age. It set itself the task of discovering an art form which was neither naturalistic nor mechanistic. It could not stomach the saccharine hearts and flowers which sentimentalized so much of Victorian decorative art and so turned to the jungle for its inspiration. It took natural forms and invested them with a dynamic barbarism. Ivy did not cling to Art Nouveau, it writhed across it. Everything twisted sinuously, even erotically. It evoked the drugged dreams of Baudelaire and the decadent excesses of Oscar Wilde's *Salome* — for which we have the illustrations by Aubrey Beardsley, himself a gilded lily of the Art Nouveau movement.

For a while, the style was triumphant, and the decorative arts embraced all that was exotic: peacocks, sirens with flowing sea-tresses, fungi, conches, all swirling like tidal sedge. It is possible to be patronizing about Art Nouveau, but hardly possible for the eye not to be delighted. Fortunately for collectors, the brief movement left behind it a wealth of

An Art Deco study of a dancer.

artifacts which will stand the test of time and remain one of the safest of investments.

Art Deco, a term derived from Arts Decoratifs, flowered in the 1920s as an expression of the cynicism of art in the aftermath of World War I. Its forms were curvilinear to start with, but unlike Art Nouveau its curves were listless, its nudes sexless. As it developed, Art Deco moved towards more angular forms expressing mechanical motion. Its materials were strap metal, tubing and stainless steel. If there is a single theme in Art Deco, it is a certain dehumanized quality — passionless, bored — in the same way that contemporary literature was peopled by the bored young things of that brittle age.

Given the present popularity of Art Deco, it is important for the collector to distinguish between it and Kitsch. This is not an easy task because the difference may only be in the eye of the beholder. If you like it, it is Art Deco; if you think it is utter garbage, it is Kitsch.

"Kitsch", in fact, is taken from the German and means "utter garbage." It has been further defined as "the debasement of refined design in popular adaptation." Mass production made the adaptation possible; quasi-art objects were manufactured for the variety store market.

Art Deco did not survive the mid-thirties. Kitsch, from which it is barely distinguishable, still dominates the novelty market. Katharine Morrison McClinton, writing in 1972 said "Art Deco Kitsch is now the craze. Most collectors today concentrate on this type of Art Deco because it is cheap and because it is fun."

Collectors should consider it only while it remains both cheap and fun. As an investment potential it is hardly possible to imagine a worse bet.

LIMITED EDITIONS

Collector plates and limited editions have blossomed into a multi-million dollar international market, one that is managed by shrewd businessmen whose job it is, like all shrewd businessmen, to maximize their sales and profits. That is what they get paid for, and anyone who sees this as an area for investment should never for one moment forget it.

Marketing strategy is to sell as much as you can of your product this year and, by dint of publicity, try to increase the number of customers next year. When next year's customers try to buy this year's plate, provided relatively few of them came onto the market, the price will go up. This is taken as evidence that the buyers of this year's plate made a good investment, a fact which is duly reported in the publications serving collectors. The result is that even fewer owners are willing to part with them, and more buyers want to get them.

The situation creates a bubble, the bursting of which I have been predicting for years, and I am still wrong! I will continue to be wrong as long as market managers can add to the total number of collectors — now believed to be over four million, world-wide.

The following is for those who have an uneasy feeling that this cannot go on forever. Wisdom begins with a clear definition of what a limited edition really is. It is a fixed, pre-stated number of something: plates, bowls, art prints or goblets. Every one is numbered and signed by the artist or craftsman, along with a guarantee by the distributor that the moulds or plates were destroyed when the run was completed. This information must be marked clearly on each piece, or indicated on a certificate accompanying it.

The total number produced is important. In a catalogue of items issued to celebrate the Silver Jubilee of Queen Elizabeth in 1977 is seen such articles as a "Reproduction 18th century clock in mahogany case with sterling silver dial, limited edition of 250," or a "Sterling silver bowl with Royal coat of arms in relief, limited edition of 25" and a "Pair of sterling silver bon-bon dishes, limited edition of 250 pairs." Those are truly limited editions. Reading on, one sees a "Child's mug with handle in Britannia silver, unlimited edition but only a small number will be produced." All these items were offered by Garrad of Regent Street, a company with an impeccable reputation. I know what the first three descriptions mean, but I do not know what the fourth means. The bon-bon dishes sold for

£625 a pair, the mug for £175. Personally I would feel much more comfortable with one pair of dishes than four mugs.

The more familiar collector plate market involves much higher production figures. I do not know the current sales of B & G Christmas Plates, but they are presumably well over a quarter of a million. At the other end of the scale few offerings fall below 10,000. This does not at all indicate that B & G plates are an inferior buy; quite the contrary, they enjoy a world-wide reputation and are far more likely to appreciate than such ephemeral properties as Elvis Presley mementos.

My best advice is to stay away from this market altogether unless:

- The "limited" nature of the piece is precisely defined to your satisfaction
- Artistic merit is sufficiently high to confer some intrinsic value of its own
- Owning the item will give you pleasure
- You are prepared to wait ten or twenty years for a profit
- If you are looking for a short-term investment, you are prepared to study the market through such publications as the *Bradford Exchange*.

If future profitability is your motive, you would be well advised to consult your dealer about possible alternatives. An item is no

Canadian Collector Plate of "Quebec Winter" by Cornelius Krieghoff.

Canadian Collector Plate of a James Keirstead painting.

more valuable simply because some marketing manager decided to offer it as a "collector plate." He does not decide what is collectible, you do, and dealers in fine china have many superb pieces on their shelves which are not offered as collector's items at all but which are far better bets for the future.

Those interested in Canadiana might profitably take a look at the Canadian Collector Plate series. This company is issuing 24 bone china plates, all illustrated by Canadian artists. World distribution will be limited to 10,000. Full details of the editions are printed on the back of each plate, with the actual number of each one clearly marked. Currently, the company has entered into an agreement with the Royal Ontario Museum to reproduce Cornelius Krieghoff's "Quebec Winter." The fact that the R.O.M. is satisfied with the colour reproduction and quality and is prepared to lend its name to the project does suggest a very legitimate venture. More information about the plate is available from the R.O.M. or about the series from Canadian Collector Plates, P.O. Box 537, Milliken, Ontario LOH 1KO.

MUSIC BOXES

Music boxes are for the elitist collector. To be sure they abound in the novelty trade and are readily available in the form of steins, jewel boxes and similar knick-knacks, but they tend to contain the same factory-made movements. No matter how modern and jolly the melodies, the link with the past is maintained by a sad,

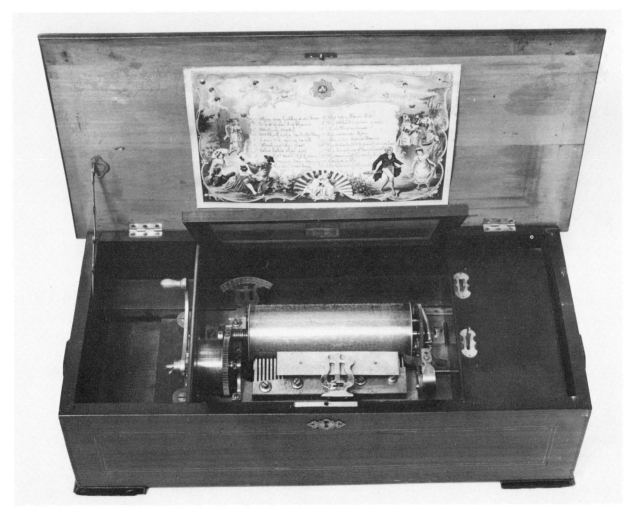

This Swiss music box plays the 20 tunes listed on the lid. Late 19th century.

nostalgic quality, the hallmark of all music boxes, which perhaps a musicologist could explain.

Legitimate collectible music boxes are doubtless still being made, but the great age was the 19th century. Original instruments from that period are unlikely to turn up at your friendly neighbourhood garage sale. In fact, the age of the music box spans less than a hundred years beginning in Switzerland in the late 1790s and effectively ending in the late 1880s when Thomas Edison invented his speaking machine. During the last decade of the 19th century, music box technology fought a valiant rearguard action. The first electrically driven model was produced in 1890, and in 1892, coin-operated instruments anticipating the juke box were installed in ice cream parlours. The automatic changer appeared in 1897, but by that time Edison's phonograph had clearly emerged as the force of the future.

It must be remembered that early music boxes were far more than novelties for the amusement of children; they were the only devices at that time for bringing recorded music into the home. Inevitably, the industry was an offshoot of watch-making, hence the strong Swiss influence. The apparatus had to be compact, precision-crafted and spring-operated. The very first models were built into watches, offered as optional additional equipment, so to speak. Morton Shulman, in *Anyone Can Make Big Money Buying Art*, speaks of complicated automatic watches of the period trading for many thousands of dollars. The field is, as he says, free of forgeries, because of the immense cost which would be involved in reproducing such intricate mechanisms today.

The same is true of virtually all early music boxes. By 1815, they had become quite the rage and were incorporated into all manner of items, such as cane tops, jewelry and snuff boxes. After this date came rapid technological improvement. The year 1850 saw the first changeable cylinder, and in 1869 we were nearly pitch-forked into the modern age by a patented device, developed by one Frank Kullrich, which would show a series of pictures through a built-in aperture, synchronized in time with the music. There is

no evidence that this primitive "boob-toob" ever actually came onto the market.

In 1879, Paillard of Geneva, one of the truly great names in music boxes, arranged a series of different cylinders on a single rotating shaft so that a number of different melodies could be played on the same machine. This would have been a major breakthrough, but for the roughly contemporary Edison invention.

Music box collectors tend to fall into two categories: those interested in ingenuity, and those seeking musical qualities. The twain do not necessarily meet. The purists are the music lovers who judge an instrument by how well and how truly it plays its melody. Parlour models of the period were capable of producing up to 400 notes and, to quote *Time/Life Encyclopedia*, "In the late 1890s, the Olympic music box was advertised with the assertion that the piano cannot produce the richness attained by the Olympia unless played by six or eight hands, and then the players must be experts."

MEMORIES OF CHILDHOOD

The survival of childhood antiques is not great. Children are not famous for the tender loving care they bestow on the objects that pass through their sticky little fingers. Toys get broken, dolls are played with to death, books are torn and scribbled in, clothes are worn out. It is a miracle anything survives at all.

The task confronting the collector, therefore, is a challenging one, and like so many general categories of collectibles it begins with a problem of selectivity. Dolls, toys and books are complete collectibles in their own right, and each of them breaks down into many sub-categories. After all, there are now well over four billion people living on this planet, and all of them were children once. The child's world is a very complete one, duplicating the adult world in almost every particular, but in miniature.

Collectibles are pioneer rocker cradles and caned high chairs, both of which sometimes turn up at country auctions; baby plates and alphabet plates are popular, as are feeding bottles and children's decorated mugs. Baby carriages known to the Victorians as perambulators — later contracted to "prams" — were often marvels of elegance and many of these also survived. There was a superstition, as I remember it, that saving such things as prams and high chairs was the best guarantee against having to use them again. To throw them out was to tempt fate, an old wives' tale which makes the task of today's collector that much easier.

Antique toys were not protected by the same superstition and are therefore a lot harder to find in good condition. They fascinate us today by reason of their high nostalgia content. We may be prejudiced, but it is hard for us to believe that they were not more exciting to yesterday's children than today's plastic artifacts, which look as though they were designed by computers (which is possible) to be played with by computers (which would be appropriate).

Those of us whose childhood dates back to before World War II (which makes us antiques but not necessarily collector's items) remember our own personal toys: hobby horses and rocking horses, train sets, tin models held together with lugs that rarely stood up to our boisterous handling, tiny merry-go-rounds, tin soldiers, alphabet blocks, ludo sets, model planes, jigsaw puzzles, marbles and yo-yos. Best of all in my memory were those long defunct whipping tops. How they ever fell from favour I shall never know. All of them are collectible today.

James Mackay in his book, *Childhood Antiques*, tells about the invention of the Teddy bear. A political cartoon in the *Washington Evening Star* on November 18, 1902, alluded to the fact that President Theodore (Teddy) Roosevelt had baulked at shooting a tiny bear cub while on a hunting expedition in the Rockies. Morris Mitchom, a toymaker, was inspired by the cartoon to produce the creature which achieved international fame as the Teddy Bear. The Ideal Toy Company made a fortune out of it, and sixty years later was commissioned by the United States Government to develop Smokey the Bear for the U.S. Forestry Service. On the way, the original Teddy spawned such offspring as Yogi Bear, Rupert Bear and the immortal Winnie-the-Pooh.

Perhaps the most charming of childhood antiques are the nursery miniatures; some were made to furnish doll's houses and others were salesmen's samples. All were perfect replicas of everyday objects made for easy portability in the salesman's sample kit. Today we are seeing a new wave of contemporary miniatures, exquisitely precise models of classic furniture, etc., made by fine craftspeople. The prices are high but not out of line with the workmanship.

Small pine armoire *from Quebec, circa 1820.*

9 Collecting for the Future

What are the collectibles of the future? Which of today's throwaways will become tomorrow's treasures? How far away is tomorrow? The only certainty is that change will be rapid and success will belong to those whose forecasts are most accurate. Here are some of my own thoughts on the subject.

1. Collect small things. Unlimited personal space is a thing of the past. We will lack storage facilities for the things we are hoping eventually to unload, and buyers of the future will have nowhere to put the stuff. People may still buy bulky things, but not many of them. The very word "collection" implies a lot of something, and the factor of display space can only become more critical as time goes on.

2. If you save what everyone else is saving, your hoard will be worth little. If you save what no one else is saving, your hoard may also be worth little. There have to be other collectors who want what you are selling. The world's largest collection of rubber duckies may be unique, but its uniqueness may mean that no one else wants it. It is therefore not just a matter of anticipating what will be rare but what collectors of the future will be looking for.

3. Think of things that will continue to exist, but not in today's form as in the following examples.

PRE-DIGITAL WATCHES AND CLOCKS

It is reasonable to assume that clocks with hands are on the way out. Well before the end of the century, all clocks will be digital, and therefore all old clocks with hands will be collectible. Good old clocks of any vintage can always be relied on to hold their price; it is the cheap alarm clocks and watches the 21st century collector will be looking for,

particularly watches because they are small. A popular low-priced brand like Timex, a company which has been marketing large numbers of new designs for a long time, are likely to be among the top-ranked collectibles of the next 100 years. They are not made to be kept as heirlooms, and right now there must be millions of them in use. By the end of the century, old Timex pre-digital watches still languishing in forgotten drawers may well number no more than 100,000 or so. That would make them perfect collectibles. If Timex are shrewd, they will introduce date coding in their watches which would front-end load the value of "first editions." Collect them now from friends. Save the boxes, too.

POCKET CALCULATORS

We may suppose that the pocket calculators pouring onto the market now in an immense variety of styles, shapes and capacities will all be made obsolete, not once but a dozen times in the next 100 years, by new-wave calculators operating on totally different principles. Today's models may well become the oil-lamps of the calculator age — very quaint, very collectible and very small.

PRE-METRIC COLLECTIBLES

However much trouble we old-timers may have in translating miles into kilometers, every year brings a new class of youngsters to whom an ounce is about as meaningful as a groat or peck. This subject is so vast that the individual pack rat must use his own imagination: foot rulers, thermometers, postal scales all have good future potential.

FOLK ART

By folk art I mean anything made by today's individual craftspeople. If some of them go on to become famous, their work will graduate to fine art; if not, it will join the anonymous treasure of folk art that is bound to become ever more precious in tomorrow's computer society. Anything made by hand will have a special cachet: textiles, pottery, craft, jewelry, metalwork, woodcarvings. Ingenuity is endless, and everything is "one-of-a-kind."

CANADIAN NATIVE ART

Inuit art has already disappeared into the galleries, and much of what is offered as Indian art originates in Taiwan. Some study is called for, but the perceptive buyer will be able to make very good investments.

PRINTED MATERIAL

Proceed with caution. Cheap paper disintegrates. The cost of preserving old comic books, no matter how valuable, may prove prohibitive. Save only things that are very well printed on very good paper. Corporation annual reports are excellent, especially corporations that will go out of business sometime in the near future as a result of making obsolescent goods.

One aspect of the limited editions market is the literature. This is a high markup commodity, and the advertising material is often superb — wonderful graphics on high-quality paper. Franklin Mint literature is so good that it can hardly fail eventually to be worth more than the articles it advertises. Sotheby Parke Bernet's publication *Preview*, an illustrated guide to their future world-wide sales, may well be the world's most collectible publication. It is a masterpiece of the printer's art, and the paper is good for centuries.

AUTOGRAPHS

This one has immense potential for future appreciation. Don't bother with signatures on cards. Celebrities cannot be blamed for being slightly resentful that your only interest in them is the potential resale value of their signatures. The least you can do is to infer that you care about them as individuals. For example, first see the play and then ask the stars to sign the programme. Make sure the programme is dated; later on you won't be able to remember what year it was. If you are collecting recording artists, buy the record and ask them to sign it. Have authors sign their books, and ask politicians to sign programmes of meetings they have addressed which you have attended. In each instance, file the signed programme with press reviews covering the event, but don't use paper clips or glue to hold them together, because rust and paper deterioration are the inevitable results over time.

You can have fun with this one. Your own ability to predict the future will be revealed by how well you anticipate greatness. Your collection of Broadbentiana will be worth a fortune if he ever does become Canada's Prime Minister; your collection of Joe Clarkiana will be worth little if he does not get a second chance. Given the Canadian practice of villifying its Prime Ministers while they are alive and collecting them when they are dead and gone, Trudeau, who surely will be out of office by the end of the century, is an excellent bet for future collectibility. If he does become Secretary General of the United Nations as his recent denial would seem to indicate, the market in Trudeauiana is going to be healthy indeed.

BOOKS ABOUT COLLECTIBLES

I would like to think that this book is a future collector's item in its own right, but I doubt it — it is too general for that. The valuable books of the future will all date from the Golden Age when much of the original research on Canadiana was being done, much of it by collectors who were far from being writers and finally had to act as their own publishers. Many are amateurish mimeographed editions, some are coffee table books, still others are professionally researched studies by specialists.

Beautifully made coffee table books like those of Donald Blake Webster and Howard Pain are likely to be reprinted for decades to come. It is the first editions, therefore, which will achieve exceptional values. Books like Loris Russell's study of early Canadian lighting and the Burnhams' book on textiles, because of their specialization, may possibly not stay in print and will become extremely valuable for the good reason that no one will ever do all that research again.

That leaves the privately printed books, such as Jim Herr's guides to Ontario Sodawater bottles, the Hogans' book of cans and containers, Jean Frances' books of Canadian dolls and John Barclay's *Canadian Fruit Jar Report*. They are either long since sold out, or are available only from the authors. They are not likely to be reprinted.

PHOTOGRAPHY

A pleasant hobby and a sure-bet future collectible is to use your own camera to record the changing face of your own town. Take before and after shots of buildings as they are demolished; ask your local wrecker to keep you informed. The moment you become sensitive to the changes that take place in every town you will find much of interest to occupy you, and the result will be historical documents of great value for the future. Make notes regarding every shot, especially dates, and save the negatives.

*   *   *   *

The foregoing is offered, not as a record of my own predictions so much as an attempt to focus on the kind of thinking the collector with an eye on the future has to do. What do you think is going to happen? If, for example, you are convinced that all our lakes are going to be destroyed by acid rain, it would be a good idea to collect fishing tackle, memorabilia of a forgotten sport. My conclusions may not be the same as yours. In fact, I hope they are not, because if we all collect the same things, they are not going to be worth very much at all.

The final element is time. The one characteristic that most collectors share is

impatience. It is going to be a long time before Canadian Centennial collectibles of 1967 begin to appreciate to any important extent. We are little more than the same span of time away from the year 2000. Wisdom dictates that when considering collectibles of the future, we think not even in terms of our children but of our grandchildren.

*   *   *   *

For expert opinions on more orthodox antiques and collectibles, I invited two of Canada's most distinguished auction houses to give us their views on investing for the future. The first comes from Christopher Edmondson, President of Phillips Ward-Price, Toronto and Montreal.

In the late 1960s and early 70s some interesting phenomena manifested themselves in Europe, particularly in Britain, stemming from an insidious household word "inflation." People saw the purchasing power of their money being eroded and the income from their savings not keeping pace with this erosion, with the attendant result that people's net worth very often was less at the end of the year than at the beginning.

The traditional investment vehicles became unpredictable, and people started to look to other, more tangible areas to spread their portfolios, primarily real estate and commercial bonds. People also saw opportunities in the movable property field, such as stamps, coins, paintings, jewelry, etc. After all, why not have the best of both worlds, an easily liquidated asset, and something that could be enjoyed at the same time.

Collectors, of course, have been around since the dawn of civilization, developing their collections of aesthetic pleasure. But now a new breed of "collector" has joined their ranks, the investor.

The inevitable happened. The law of supply and demand dictated that prices would go up and the ordinary collector was forced to look at other collecting fields as they were priced out of the more traditional areas.

For instance, as the collector found quality Old Master paintings denied to him, he looked at a later era, the Victorian period. Works of semi-neglected artists of stature suddenly came into demand. The pre-Raphaelites, like Burne-Jones, Solomon, Rosetti and Strudwick, are classic examples.

A similar buying pattern is developing in Canada, and there is now every evidence that more and more Canadians are emulating their European counterparts for the same reason and with the same effect. Canadian art of the highest quality has seen a remarkable mushrooming in price and is, in our

This 20th century piece of folk art was carved by an unknown but talented carver.

opinion, still undervalued as a result of a measure of indifference on the part of the international market which is inexplicable and almost bound to change.

Fine and scarce Canadian furniture, early folk art, decoys and Indian trade silver certainly, in our view, have not reached a peak at time of writing. Indeed, we anticipate a boom in these areas as the major collections now formed begin to turn around.

However, Canadians are not confining themselves to Canadiana. There is considerable activity in all international fields with perhaps the fine quality, small, portable items showing the most headway.

The result of all this activity is that, as the more rare items are being forced up in price, the buyer with less money to spend, is looking to lesser known artists and new collecting fields.

What then of the future? One of the most frequently asked questions is: "What should I buy as a good investment?" It is not easy to second-guess the future, but there is one golden rule which never changes: buy the best quality you can afford from the most reputable source. We at Phillips Ward-Price believe that you cannot, and should not, promote any art work or collectible on the basis of its investment

potential, rather that you should buy it only because you like it and can afford it.

As far as investment potential is concerned, it is true that if you drew a graph of the price rise in quality works of art, it will have kept ahead of inflation in the medium term. However, the sharp inflationary rise in price of works of art is a relatively recent phenomenon, and who knows for sure whether, or for how long, the pace will continue.

As a collector, only your discernment and gut instinct will tell you that.

The second and equally valid view is the contribution of N. L. Young, Director of Antiques and Art, Maynards Auctioneers, Vancouver and Toronto.

Maynards offers a wide variety of antiques and collectibles through their auctions. From Elizabethan oak furniture to Royal Doulton figurines, from Oriental porcelains to antique needlework, the bidders come in search of good buys. The most important point when collecting and investing for the novice bidder should be age and quality. Too many first-time buyers equate the auction market with the stock market, but the world does not rise or fall on the demand for Georgian furniture the way it does for petroleum products. Certainly, a piece of Georgian furniture, say a set of dining room chairs, may be seen as an investment. But remember that good sets may be scarce, and one must be prepared to pay a very high price. One may find bargains, but often this will be due to the fact that incredible restoration will be necessary. Knowledgeable collectors and top dealers are often reluctant to purchase heavily restored goods. If the set of chairs is kept for a year and again sent to auction, the investment potential may be negligible after you take into consideration the sale price less commissions and other deductions. The auction market is not designed for rapid turn-over so much as long term appreciation.

A knowledgeable buyer will research the current auction market before purchasing goods which may be faddish. We would recommend that buyers stay with the tried and true: good, old oriental rugs; 18th and 19th century furniture; quality Continental and Oriental porcelains (Meissen, Worcester, Crown Derby and Imari pieces); English sterling, etc.

There are certain markets in Canada in which a buyer may still make a good investment: 19th century bronzes, antique needlework, first-edition books, watercolours, etc. European collectors, whose cultural heritage goes further back, have been quicker to recognize good pieces which Canadian buyers are only now beginning to collect. These include Art Nouveau and Art Deco goods, especially Studio pottery from the English Arts and Crafts Movement, Loetz glass, Lalique jewelery, etc.

It would be my opinion that Canadian collectors are either conservative in their tastes on the one hand, or liable to pay too much for unproven "collectibles" on the other. While it may be enjoyable to accumulate a collection of North American pressed glass medicine bottles, the owner can hardly expect to make a fortune on their resale.

One important area which Canadian buyers are still neglecting, and for which high prices are being realized in New York sales, are our native goods or ethnographic materials. The West Coast used to be rich in carved masks, poles, rattles, blankets, etc. from the Kwatiutl, Haida and Tlingit tribes. We would regard them as an excellent investment, because they are artistic, hand-crafted and historical.

People interested in antiques as an investment should certainly subscribe to journals on antiques, attend as many auctions in their area as they can and bone up on their chosen fields by reading the many fine antique and art books currently available.

The drawing room of The Grange, Toronto, Ontario, restored in the Regency style. The harp, rosewood pianoforte and cut crystal girandoles on the mantle are English. The "Grecian" couch is simulated rosewood, while the classical design chimney looking glass has a gilt frame.

10 Antique Hunting Across Canada

The only way to gain any real knowledge of antiques is by looking at them and, if at all possible, by handling them. I could talk till the cows come home about cut glass and how it is different from its imitations, but you would not learn as much as you would in five minutes spent with a good dealer who invited you to look at the way the light catches it, feel the weight, observe the depth and sharpness of the cuts, listen to the ringing tone when you "ping" it, and then compare it with a 5 & 10¢ store imitation.

A book can only tell you "about" antiques. The richness of patina, the unique smoothness of satin glass, the smell of old beeswax, the weight of ancient sadirons, the feel of old textiles, these can only be experienced from direct contact with the object itself, and if that contact takes place under the guidance of a reasonably knowledgeable person, the richer the experience will be.

Wealth, finally, lies not in ownership but knowledge. Few of us can afford to assemble great collections; we must indulge our passion sparingly, and the knowledge we acquire from the things we actually buy comes all too slowly. Fortunately, by way of consolation, even the poorest of us have access to the riches of the past thanks to those who care about such things and have made their care available to the rest of us. There is scarcely a community anywhere that does not have its local museum, its little antique store, its fairs and flea markets, and these are staffed for the most part by volunteers, people who have a great love for old things and want to share that love.

Most of our cities have one or more splendid old houses that have been lovingly restored, furnished in period style and opened to the public. These too are well worth a visit, but they do tend to leave one with a sense of frustration. Understandably you are not permitted to wander at will among so many irreplaceable treasures. These may be glimpsed on the other side of rope barriers, and what information you get may come only from a costumed student for whom this is a summer job. He or she is hardly in a position to answer questions which are not already covered in a canned tour guide spiel.

Pioneer villages are a better bet. There your sense of the past is deepened and made more vivid by being involved rather than just spectating. The costumed staff is likely to be more permanent; very often they are skilled craftspeople who are sharing an authentic way of life with you.

By all means visit Dundurn Castle when you are in Hamilton, or Rutherford House when you go to Edmonton, and most certainly spend as much time as you can afford in pioneer villages, but the antique lover bent on self education will make a point of never missing a local museum. The crowds are smaller — in fact you may have the place to yourself — and the curator will be delighted to show you around, let you look at and possibly handle individual items, load you with local folklore and leave you feeling that this must be the most delightful of occupations.

The following list of important places to visit while antique hunting across Canada is arranged alphabetically by province. It cannot hope to be complete, but it will give you a good start in acquiring knowledge, enjoyment and a sense of Canada's past. Many smaller institutions are open only during the summer months; these are marked S.O. Larger museums and pioneer villages frequently operate all year round; these are marked A.Y.

ALBERTA

Museums

Andrew. District Museum, Highway 45 at 815. A.Y. Regional pioneer artifacts.

Banff. Luxton Museum, 1 Birch Avenue. A.Y. Furniture, pioneer memorabilia.

Calgary. Glenbow Museum, 9th Avenue and 1st Street S.E. A.Y. Museum, art gallery, archives.
   Heritage Park Museum, 1900 Heritage Drive S.W. S.O. Artifacts of early Alberta.

Cochrane. Cochrane Ranch. S.O. Old ranch site.

Debolt. Pioneer Museum. S.O. Old tools, furniture and photographs.

Delburne. Anthony Henday Museum. S.O. Historic material and archives.

Drumheller. Homestead Antique Museum Dinosaur Trail, ½ mile west of Drumheller. S.O. Pioneer artifacts and photographs.

Edmonton. Dolls and Costume Museum. A.Y. Outstanding collection of classic dolls.
   John Walter Historic Site, 10627 93 Avenue, south of 105th Street bridge. S.O. Early history of province.
   Provincial Museum and Archives, 12845 102nd Avenue. A.Y. History of Alberta from earliest times.

Lethbridge. Sir Alexander Galt Museum, west end of 5th Avenue. A.Y. Canadiana of late 19th century.

Red Deer. Red Deer and District Museum, Recreation Centre, 45th Street and 47A Avenue. A.Y. Furniture, tools, photographs.

Pioneer Villages

Willingdon. Willingdon Historic Village. S.O. Reconstructed pioneer settlement.

Historic Parks

Elk Island National Park. Ukrainian Cultural Village, Fort Saskatchewan. S.O. Accurately restored pre-1930 village with wide array of handmade and manufactured artifacts.

Houses

Edmonton. Rutherford House, 11153 Saskatchewan Drive. A.Y. Restored 1911 home of a former Premier of Alberta. Furnished in period. Vast collection of Canadiana.

BRITISH COLUMBIA

Museums

Ashcroft. Ashcroft Museum, Railway Avenue and Third Street. S.O. Early tools, lamps, farm implements.

Cranbrook. Railway Museum, 1 Van Horne Street North. A.Y. Restored CPR coach, "The Argyle," displays of railway china, glass and silver.

Cumberland. Cumberland Museum, Chamber of Commerce Building, Dunsmuir Avenue and 4th Street. S.O. Old photographs and early surgical instruments.

Duncan. British Columbia Forest Museum, 2892 Drinkwater, 1 mile north of Duncan on the Trans-Canada Highway. S.O. Ninety-acre outdoor museum with historic logging equipment and steam locomotives.

Fort Langley. Centennial Museum, 9135 King Street. A.Y. Pioneer artifacts and archives.

Golden. Golden and District Museum, 11th Avenue at 13th Street. S.O. Pioneer collections and photographs.

Hudson's Hope. Historical Museum, Beattie Drive and Fredette Avenue. S.O. Logging memorabilia.

Mission. Mission Museum, 33201 2nd Avenue. A.Y. Bottles, period rooms and archives.

Nanaimo. Centennial Museum, 100 Cameron Road. A.Y. Mining and pioneer collection. Archives.

North Vancouver. North Shore Museum and Archives, 617 West 23rd Street. A.Y. Photographs, early industry and private collections.

Vancouver. British Columbia Museum of Medicine, Academy of Medicine Building, 1807 West 10th Avenue. A.Y. Medical material dating back to earliest times.

Old Hastings Mill Store Museum, 1575 Alma Road. A.Y. Pioneer relics, furniture, pictures and maps housed in an old (1865) store.

Victoria. British Columbia Provincial Museum, 675 Belleville Street. A.Y. History of British Columbia.

Metchosin School Museum, 611 Happy Valley Road. A.Y. Photos and displays of pioneer items.

Old Craigflower School Museum, 2765 Admirals Road. An 1855 classroom, stagecoach and farm artifacts.

Point Ellice House Museum, 2616 Pleasant Street. A.Y. Household goods, furnishings, and costumes.

White Rock. City Museum, 14970 Marine Drive. A.Y. Archival history of the district.

Pioneer Villages

Burnaby. Heritage Village, 4900 Deer Lake Avenue — Canada Way near Gilpin Street, at the Sperling exit off Highway 1. A.Y. Village street reconstruction (circa 1900), store, blacksmith, Chinese herbalist, school, etc.

Dawson Creek. South Peace Pioneer Village, 1636 94 Avenue, 3 miles out of town on the Edmonton Highway. S.O. Original log homes, churches, blacksmith and a trapper's cabin on a 25-acre site.

Historic Parks

Barkerville. Historic Park, Highway 26, 52 miles west of Quesnel. A.Y. Restored gold rush town of the 1890s.

Harrison Mills. Kilby Historic Park, 215 Kilby Road. A.Y. Reconstructed general store of the 1920s.

Fort Langley. National Historic Park, 23433 Mavis. A.Y. Fur trade post from the 1840-58 era, period furniture, costumed guides.

Fort St. James. National Historic Park. A.Y. Six buildings furnished to the period of 1896.

Heritage Village, Burnaby, British Columbia.

Fort Steele. Fort Steele Historic Park, 10 miles north-east of Cranbrook on Highway 93/95. A.Y. Restored turn-of-century buildings, steam locomotives and rail cars.

Houses

New Westminster. Irving House Historic Centre, 302 Royal Avenue. A.Y. Fourteen-room pioneer home (1864-1890), fully furnished.

Victoria. Helmcken House, 638 Elliott Street, Heritage Court. A.Y. Historic home restored to period of the 1860s; includes medical instruments of the period.

MANITOBA

Museums

Dauphin. Fort Dauphin Museum, 140 Jackson Street at 4th Avenue S.W. S.O. Recreation of fur trade fort and 1892 pioneer home.

Elkhorn. Manitoba Automobile Museum, Highway 1. S.O. Over 90 automobiles, 1908-1958.

The formal late Victorian parlour in Irving House, New Westminster, B.C. The piano, by Mason & Risch Ltd. of Toronto, is from an earlier period.

Gardenton. Ukrainian Museum, 65 miles south-east of Winnipeg on Highways 59 and 209. S.O. Clothes, household items, equipment.

Langruth. Heritage Museum. S.O. Reconstructed pioneer rooms with period furniture.

La Riviere. Archibald Museum, Highway 3, 2 miles east and 4 miles north of La Riviere. S.O. Nellie McClung lived in this 1878 log home, now restored.

Swan River. Swan Valley Museum, Highway 10, 1 mile north of Swan River. S.O. Five buildings house the collection of pioneer artifacts.

Treherne. Treherne Museum, Highway 12 just south of the Pool Elevator on Vanzile Street. S.O. Contains a gun collection, clocks, lamps, swords, etc.

Victoria Beach. The Ateah Museum, Highway 59. A.Y. Furniture, stoves, pots and pans, dishes, gramophones, bottles, guns and tools.

Whitemouth. Municipal Museum, 70 miles east of Winnipeg on Highway 44, Whitemouth Community Grounds. S.O. Restored pioneer home with antique farm machinery and implements.

Winnipeg. Museum of St. Boniface, 494 Avenue Tache. A.Y. Winnipeg's oldest building (1846) houses the largest collection of French-Canadian and Metis artifacts in western Canada.

Manitoba Museum of Man, 190 Rupert Avenue. A.Y. Provincial history from earliest times.

Museum of St. James-Assiniboia, 3180 Portage Avenue. Pioneer displays, artifacts, vintage dental equipment.

Lower Fort Garry, Selkirk, Manitoba.

Pioneer Villages

Austin. Homesteader's Village, 2 miles south of the junction of Highways 1 and 34, west of Austin. S.O. Home of Canada's largest agricultural museum. Huge collection of early farm tools and domestic items, such as shaving mugs, clocks, gramophones and textiles. The village includes a church, log school, post office, grist mill and blacksmith's shop.

Beausejour. Broken-Beau Historical Society Museum Village, Centennial Park. S.O. Several completely restored buildings and a fine collection of pioneer materials.

Portage La Prairie. Fort de la Reine Museum, Highway 1A, 2 miles east of Portage La Prairie. S.O. Reconstructed fort originally built by La Verendrye in 1738. The village includes log homestead, Manitoba's "Farm of the Century," a church and a schoolhouse. William Van Horne's 1882 official business railway car is here.

Steinbach. Mennonite Village, Highway 12, 1½ miles north of Steinbach. S.O. The complex houses a complete reconstruction of Prairie Mennonite pioneer life with log huts, barns, church and Canada's only wind-powered grist mill. Magnificent eatery of delicious Mennonite food. Books, furniture, clocks and tools.

Historic Parks

Selkirk. Lower Fort Garry Historical Park, 20 miles north of Winnipeg on Highway 9. S.O. Complex of historic buildings restored to the years 1835-1875. One of the oldest stone fur trading posts in North America. Costumed staff and craftspeople.

Houses

Souris. Hillcrest Museum, 26 Crescent East. S.O. Historic home of unique architecture, with furnished period rooms and pioneer materials.

Virden. Pioneer Home Museum, 390 King Street West. A.Y. Brick home built in 1888, completely refurnished.

Seven Oaks House in Winnipeg, Manitoba. In the foreground is an early can opener with a press and sausage maker behind. A coffee mill, butter bowl and paddles and butter print sit on the cupboard at the left rear, and a scale hangs above it.

Winnipeg. Dalnavert-Macdonald House, 61 Carlton Street. A.Y. Restored Victorian home of one of the former Premiers of Manitoba. Superbly furnished in period style. The restoration was carried out by the Manitoba Historical Society.

Seven Oaks House, Rupertsland Avenue East, 1½ blocks from Main Street, West Kildonan. S.O. The oldest house in Manitoba, built in 1851 by John Inkster. Constructed of oak logs, it contains furniture and household articles of the period. Every room an antique lover's paradise.

NEW BRUNSWICK

Museums

Buctouche. Kent Museum, 150 Convent Street. S.O. Century-old restored convent.

Campobello. Roosevelt Summer Home, Campobello Island, Welsh Pool, N.B. S.O. Franklin D. Roosevelt summer cottage and estate.

Edmundston. Madawaska Regional Museum, 195 boul Hebert. S.O. Presents a story of northwestern New Brunswick.

Gagetown. Queens County Museum, on Route 102. S.O. Restored home of Father of Confederation, Sir Leonard Tilley.

Grand Falls. Historical Museum, 150 Court Street. S.O. Local historical artifacts.

Hampton. Kings County Historical Society Museum, Centennial building, Route 121, 20 miles north of Saint John. S.O. Local historical artifacts.

Hopewell Cape. Antique Car Museum, one mile from The Rocks. S.O. Historical automobiles.

Mactaquac. Antique Arms Museum, Route 105, 15 miles west of Fredericton. S.O. Antique arms from 1640: matchlocks and flint-locks of the 1700s through percussions of the 1800s to modern firearms. Only old-fashioned shooting gallery in eastern Canada.

Moncton. Moncton Museum, Mountain Road at Belleview Avenue. S.O. History of area settlers from the 18th century to present day.

New Denmark. New Denmark Memorial Museum. Household articles, documents and machinery belonging to early Danish settlers.

Oromocto. Gagetown Military Museum, Base Gagetown. A.Y. Royal Canadian Dragoons and Black Watch artifacts and exhibits.

Richibucto. Richibucto River Museum, Route 11 Rexton, second floor of the old Post Office. S.O. Local history.

Rogersville. G.M. & C. Antique Museum, Route 126. S.O. Antique cars, guns and household appliances.

Saint John. Barbour's General Store (1867), King Street East and Carmarthen. S.O. Restored general store stocked with merchandise of the period.

The New Brunswick Museum, 277 Douglas Avenue. A.Y. Canada's oldest museum, home of the important John Clarence Webster collection of pictorial material, books, manuscripts and documents relating to Canada's development.

St. Martins. Quaco Museum and Library. S.O. Historical exhibits, archival and gene-alogical material.

St. Stephen. Charlotte County Historical Society Museum, 443 Milltown Boulevard. S.O. Artifacts illustrating Loyalist beginnings in the area.

Shediac. Sportsman's Museum, Route 16, 8 miles east of Shediac. S.O. Specializing in antique sporting equipment.

Tabusintac. Tabusintac Museum, Route 11. S.O. Work implements used by farmers and woodsmen in the area.

Pioneer Villages

Caraquet. Acadian Historical Village, Route 11, 5½ miles west of Caraquet between Caraquet and Grande-Anse. S.O. Located on 2800 acre site, the Acadian Village presents the history of a people tested and moulded by expulsion from their homes.

Hopewell Cape. Albert County Museum, off Route 114. S.O. Historic complex of five buildings displaying old handwork, tools and marine antiques.

Kings Landing. Kings Landing Historical Settlement, off Trans-Canada Highway, 23 miles west of Fredericton. S.O. Sixty buildings on a 300 acre site and costumed staff of more than 100 persons depict the lifestyles of a community of the Saint John River Valley between 1780 and the end of the 19th century.

Drying cod in the old way at Acadian Village, near Caraquet, New Brunswick.

The restored saw mill at Kings Landing Historical Settlement, Kings Landing, New Brunswick.

Historic Parks

Newcastle. Macdonald Farm Historic Park, 18 miles north of Newcastle on Route 11. S.O. Georgian stone house (1820) restored with period New Brunswick furniture.

Houses

Dorchester. Keillor House, Route 6. S.O. Circa 1813 house restored with antique furnishings.

NEWFOUNDLAND

Museums

Bonavista. Bonavista Museum. S.O. Historic items of local interest.

Cape Bonavista Lighthouse, S.O. Ancient lighthouse restored to 1870 vintage.

Durrell. Durrell Museum, Arm Lads' Brigade Armoury. S.O. Specializing in artifacts of World War I.

Ferryland. Ferryland Museum, southern shore, Ferryland. S.O. General history in old courthouse.

Gander. Aviation Exhibit, International Airport. A.Y. Unique exhibition depicting the province's role in transatlantic aviation from 1919 to 1939. Open 24 hours daily, 7 days a week.

Pleasantville. Quidi Vidi Battery, Quidi Vidi, St. John's. S.O. Military reconstruction to 1815 period.

St. John's. Commissariat House, Forest Road and King's Bridge. A.Y. Offices and private quarters restored and furnished to 1839 period.

Naval and Military Museum, Confederation Building, 11th floor. A.Y. Naval and military history of Newfoundland up to World War 1.

The Newfoundland Museum, 282 Duckworth Street. A.Y. Three floors of exhibits depicting Newfoundland history and culture.

Twillingate. Twillingate Museum. S.O. Local history in old Anglican rectory.

NOVA SCOTIA

Museums

Balmoral Mills. Grist mill, off Route 6 on Route 311. S.O. Operating grist mill and museum.

Bridgewater. Des Brisay Museum and Park, 130 Jubilee Road. A.Y. Oldest municipally owned museum collection in Nova Scotia.

Clementsport. St. Edward's Church Museum. S.O. Built like a ship of hand-hewn timbers. Erected 1797, now houses local history collection.

Dartmouth. Dartmouth Heritage Museum, 100 Wyse Road. A.Y. Display in honour of Joseph Howe in his re-created study.

Halifax. Nova Scotia Museum, 1747 Summer Street. A.Y. Headquarters for a complex of branch museums throughout Nova Scotia. Superb collection.

Province House, Granville Street. A.Y. Canada's oldest provincial legislative building.

La Have. Fort Point Museum. S.O. Site of 1632 Acadian settlement.

Margaree. Museum of Cape Breton Heritage. S.O. Household items, arts and crafts including old Scottish, Indian and Acadian work.

Parkdale. Parkdale-Maplewood Museum, reached from New Germany off Route 10. S.O. Excellent Nova Scotia books, glass and textiles.

St. Ann's. Giant MacAskill Highland Pioneers Museum. S.O. Operated by the Gaelic College of Celtic Folk Art. Related to Scottish settlers in the district.

Tatamagouche. Sunrise Trail Museum. S.O. Local historical material and memorabilia of Anna Swan, the Nova Scotia giant.

Wolfville. Historic Museum, Main Street beside William Park. S.O. New England and Loyalist artifacts.

Yarmouth. County Historical Society Museum, 22 Collins Street. A.Y. Includes Victorian sitting room, mid 19th century rooms and blacksmith shop.

Firefighter's Museum, 451 Main Street. A.Y. Old firefighting equipment and machines.

Pioneer Villages

Iona. Nova Scotia Highland Village Museum, on Route 223 at Grand Narrows. S.O. Several buildings devoted to life of early Scottish settlers.

Sherbrooke. Sherbrooke Village. S.O. Late 19th century lumbering, shipbuilding and mining community restored in period.

Historic Parks

Annapolis Royal. Fort Anne National Historic Park, 295 St. George Street. S.O. Site of 1635 Acadian settlement.

Halifax. Citadel Historic Park, Halifax Citadel. A.Y. Army museum and the anthropological collection of the Nova Scotia Museum.

Grand Pre. National Historic Park. S.O. Reconstructed Acadian chapel and museum.

Louisbourg. National Historic Park. S.O. Canada's largest historic reconstruction project involving restoration of about one-fifth of the Fortress and old town enclosed by the defences. Built in 1740 and re-created in period.

Port Royal. National Historic Park. S.O. Site of 1603 Acadian settlement.

Houses

Annapolis Royal. McNamara House, Historic Waterfront, Lower St. George Street. S.O. Restored 1790 home.

O'Dell Inn and Tavern, Historic Waterfront, Lower St. George Street. S.O. Restored to 19th century era.

Granville Ferry. North Hills House. S.O. Superb restoration in period of 1800 home.

Hantsport. Churchill House and Museum, Main Street. S.O. This 1860 house contains an outstanding collection of shipbuilding artifacts.

Liverpool. Simeon Perkins House. S.O. Built in 1766. Furnished in period.

Macpherson Mills. Mill and farm homestead. S.O. Water powered grist mill and restored farm home.

Maitland. Lawrence House, on Route 215. S.O. Restored 1874 home furnished in period.

Mount Uniacke. Uniacke House, Mount Uniacke, Hant's County. S.O. Stately colonial style home built in 1813. Features original Uniacke furnishings.

New Ross. Ross Farm, Route 12 between Kenville and Chester Basin. S.O. Restored 19th century farm and implements.

Pictou. McCulloch House. S.O. Museum and 1860 home partly furnished in period.

Shelburne. Ross-Thompson House, Charlotte Lane. S.O. A Loyalist era store and home. Contains period furniture and merchandise.

Sydney. Cossit House. S.O. Restored 1787 residence. The oldest house in Sydney.

Windsor. Haliburton Memorial Museum, Windsor. S.O. Former home of Thomas Chandler Haliburton, built in 1836. Restored and furnished in period.

ONTARIO

Museums

Adolphustown. United Empire Loyalist Museum, Highway 33, 1 mile east of the Glenora Ferry. S.O. Artifacts and displays illustrating Loyalist emigration to Ontario.

A dining room of the 1845-50 period at Upper Canada Village. The Greek "klismos" style chairs are of Canadian manufacture. The Non-Pareil stove was made by Morrison & Manning of Troy, New York.

Barrie. Sincoe County Museum, 5 miles north on Highway 26, next to Springwater Park. A.Y Pioneer artifacts.

Belleville. Hastings County Museum, 257 Bridge Street East. A.Y. Restored Victorian mansion modelled on the chateaux of France. Large exhibition of antique lighting fixtures.

Blind River. Timber Village Museum, east of town on Highway 17. S.O. Blacksmith shop, river boats, etc.

Bowmanville. Bowmanville Museum, 37 Silver Street. S.O. Large home of the 1860s featuring old-time store, period rooms and toys.

Brampton. Peel Museum and Art Gallery, 7 Wellington Street East. A.Y. Local pioneer life.

Campbellford. Trent River Pioneer Museum, 8 miles north on Highway 30. S.O. Eight original log buildings portraying home life of early settlers.

Cobourg. Barnum House Museum, 2 miles west of Grafton on Highway 2. S.O. Outstanding example of neoclassic architecture filled with furniture, china, and implements of early settlers.

Collingwood. Collingwood Museum, The Railway Station, Memorial Park, St. Paul's Street. A.Y. Housed in old railway station.

Cornwall. The Wood House Museum, 731 Second Street West. S.O. General Canadiana in old stone building.

Dundas. Historical Society Museum, 139 Park Street West. A.Y. Costumes, china, glass, toys and dolls.

Fergus. Wellington County Museum, between Fergus and Elora. A.Y. History of Wellington County.

Flesherton. South Grey Museum, Memorial Park, Highway 10. S.O. Items of local historical interest.

Forest. Forest Lambton Museum, 59 Broadway. S.O. Complete Victorian home.

Gananoque. Historical Museum, 10 King Street at the bridge. S.O. Victorian furniture in Victoria Hall. Military artifacts.

Goderich. Huron County Pioneer Museum, 110 North Street. A.Y. Twenty rooms devoted to pioneer lifestyle.

Grand Bend. Lambton Museum, Highway 21. A.Y. Pioneer history of Lambton County.

Jordan. Historical Museum of the Twenty, Twenty Mile Creek, Main Street, Jordan. S.O. Early memorabilia in three old houses.

Kingston. Murney Tower Museum, Barrie and King Street. S.O. Martello tower dating from 1846 houses the historical museum of the area.

Kleinburg. McMichael Canadian Collection, off Highway 400 at Kleinburg. A.Y. Not antiques but a fabulous collection of Group of Seven paintings set in massive buildings of stone and immense rough-hewn timbers.

Lindsay. Victoria County Historical Museum, 435 Kent Street West. S.O. Displays of 19th century Canadian glass.

Little Current. Little Current-Howland Centennial Museum, Highway 68 at Sheguiandah, south of Little Current. S.O. Log houses, granary and blacksmith shop.

London. Labatt Pioneer Brewery, 150 Simcoe Street. S.O. Reconstruction of pioneer brewery.
    Royal Canadian Regiment Museum, Oxford and Elizabeth Streets. A.Y. Exhibits in historic Wolseley Hall.

Milton. Halton Regional Museum, Kelso Conservation Area, 6 miles northwest of Milton. A.Y. Eight pioneer buildings. Outstanding lighting collection, from rush lights to Coleman lamps.
    Ontario Agricultural Museum, Highway 401, Interchange 39, 3 miles west of Milton. A.Y. Early agricultural implements.

Mississauga. Bradley House Museum, south off Highway 2 on Meadow Wood Road at Orr Road. S.O. Restored 1830 home. Exhibits recall early 19th century pioneer life.

Niagara-on-the-Lake. Niagara Fire Museum, King Street. S.O. Fire equipment 1816-1926.
    Niagara Historical Society Museum, 43 Castlereagh Street. A.Y. Ontario's oldest historical museum.

North Bay. North Bay and Area Museum, Riverbend Road. S.O. Relics of rail, lumber and steamboat eras.

Ottawa. National Museum of Man, Metcalfe and McLeod Streets. A.Y. Permanent exhibition dealing with the history and heritage of the average Canadian. The Museum features a more or less non-stop series of special exhibitions of Canadiana in all its forms.

Penetanguishene. Historical Naval and Military Establishments, Penetanguishene Bay. S.O. Seventeen restored buildings in old naval depot.

Port Carling. Port Carling Pioneer Museum, town centre, Island Park, by the locks. S.O. Pioneer history of the town.

Port Colborne. Historical and Marine Museum, 280 King Street. S.O. Marine artifacts. Excellent collection of early glassware. Some good cranberry.

Renfrew. McDougall Mills Museum, O'Brien Park, Arthur Avenue. S.O. An 1855 grist mill with pioneer artifacts.

St. Catharines. St. Catharines Historical Museum, 343 Merritt Street. A.Y. Welland Canal and War of 1812 relics.

St. Mary's. St. Mary's District Museum, 177 Church Street South. S.O. Old stone house with pioneer artifacts.

St. Thomas. Elgin County Pioneer Museum, 32 Talbot Street. A.Y. Canadiana in an 1849 pioneer physician's home.

Southampton. Bruce County Museum, 33 Victoria Street. S.O. Complex of buildings housing pioneer and Great Lakes shipping memorabilia.

Stoney Creek. Battlefield Museum, signposted from Highway 20. S.O. Handsome 1795 settler's home furnished in the style of 1830. Battle memorabilia.

Strathroy. Strathroy Middlesex Museum, 84 Oxford Street. A.Y. Housed in stately 1871 Victorian mansion.

Sudbury. Copper Cliff Museum, Balsam Street (Copper Cliff). S.O. Antiques in an early settler's cabin.

Flour Mill Heritage Museum, 514 Notre Dame Boulevard. S.O. Antique furniture, handtools and weapons.

Thunder Bay. Old Fort William, south of Broadway Avenue on King Road. S.O. Forty reconstructed buildings including quarters for blacksmith, armourer, tinsmith, cooper, carpenter and hospital.

Thunder Bay Museum, 219 May Street South. S.O. Pioneer, marine and military memorabilia.

Toronto. Royal Ontario Museum, Canadiana Building, 14 Queen's Park Crescent West. A.Y. The province's best collection of early Canadian room settings, silver, coins, medals, furniture, glassware, maps and paintings.

Todmorden Mills Museum, 67 Pottery Road. S.O. Nineteenth century mill site with two restored pre-Confederation houses and an old brewery.

Windsor. Hiram Walker Historical Museum, 254 Pitt Street West. A.Y. Local artifacts in an 1811 Georgian house.

Williamstown. Glengarry Pioneer Museum, town centre. Loyalist furniture and artifacts.

Woodstock. Oxford Museum, City Square. A.Y. Original City Hall built in 1851. Extensive collection of furniture and memorabilia.

Pioneer Villages

Doon. Doon Pioneer Village, Blair Road north off Highway 401 near Kitchener. S.O. Sixty acre complex with several reconstructed buildings displaying pioneer memorabilia.

Essex. Southwestern Ontario Heritage Village, 6 miles south of Essex on County Road 23, Arner Town Line. S.O. Fifty-four acres with 8 historic structures, a railway station and schoolhouse.

Huntsville. Muskoka Pioneer Village, Memorial Park, Brunel Road, adjacent to the high school. S.O. A dozen pioneer buildings on a wooded hillside.

Keene. Century Village, 10 miles south-east of Peterborough, 2 miles north of Keene at Lang. S.O. Fourteen restored buildings including a store, shingle mill, smithy, inn and cider barn.

Morrisburg. Upper Canada Village, 7 miles east of Morrisburg on Highway 2. S.O. A treasure house of Canadiana — all in original setting, working order and manned by craftspeople and guides in period costumes. Impossible to do justice to in one day.

Rockton. Wentworth Pioneer Village, north off Highway 52, north of Highway 8. S.O. Twenty-four restored buildings portray a community of the 1850s.

Toronto. Black Creek Pioneer Village, Jane and Steeles Avenue. A.Y. Re-creates the whole range of activities of a rural pioneer community in Ontario. Functioning mill, blacksmith's shop and pioneer crafts practised by villagers in period costume.

The study in Bellevue National Historic Park, Kingston, Ontario. The desk and clock are of the Regency period and the table-desk on the right dates from the reign of Queen Anne.

Houses

Amherstberg. John R. Park Homestead, Dalhousie Street. A.Y. Rare example of American Greek Revivalism in Ontario. Guests can experience the re-creation of pre-1850 lifestyle in Upper Canada.

Brantford. Bell Homestead, 94 Tutela Heights Road. A.Y. Home of Alexander Graham Bell, furnished as it was when he lived there. Many of his inventions are displayed.

Callander. Dionne Home, Highway 11 between Callander and North Bay. S.O. The original Dionne farmhouse made of logs; restored and furnished with "quint" memorabilia.

Guelph. The Colonel John McCrae Home, 102 Water Street West. S.O. Restored home of Canadian war poet.

Hamilton. Dundurn Castle, exit off Highway 403 to York Boulevard. A.Y. Nineteenth century 36 room manion restored to its former splendour as the home of Sir Allan Napier MacNab, Prime Minister of United Provinces of Canada (1854-56).

Whitehern House, 41 Jackson West at MacNab Street. A.Y. Handsome Georgian mansion containing many fine pieces of period furniture.

Kingston. Bellevue National Historic Park House, 35 Centre Street. A.Y. Sir John A. Macdonald's one-time home. Built around 1840, it has been restored and furnished with displays of Macdonald memorabilia.

Kirkfield. Mackenzie Historic Home, Highway 48 in town. A.Y. Forty room mansion reflects the life and times of the co-founder of the Canadian Northern Railway.

Kitchener/Waterloo. Woodside Historic Park, 528 Wellington Street North. One hundred year old mansion, home of William Lyon Mackenzie King. Restored in the 1890s style.

London. Eldon House, 481 Ridout Street North. S.O. London's oldest (1834) house, now a historic museum furnished in period.

The bedroom of William Lyon Mackenzie King, Laurier House, Ottawa. A mixture of periods and styles, from early to late. On the left is a prie-dieu.

The library of Mackenzie King, Laurier House, Ottawa.

The south bedroom in The Grange, Toronto, Ontario. The walnut bed was brought to the New World by a British officer stationed at Fort Henry. The Sheraton-style mahogany dressing table is of American origin.

Niagara-on-the-Lake. McFarland House, 1 mile south on the Niagara Parkway. S.O. Large Georgian brick house furnished in the style of the 1800s.

Oshawa. Henry House and Robinson House, Lakeview Park, Lakeshore Road at Simcoe Street. S.O. Two houses restored in the 1850-80 period.

Ottawa. Laurier House, 335 Laurier Avenue East. A.Y. Home of Sir Wilfrid Laurier and William Lyon Mackenzie King. Contains memorabilia of both.

Moorside, 8 miles north on Gatineau Parkway. S.O. Summer residence of Mackenzie King. The estate features an interesting collection of architectural details collected by King from demolished buildings in the capital and abroad.

Peterborough. Hutchison House, 270 Brock Street. A.Y. Nineteenth century doctor's house. Costumed guides demonstrate early crafts.

Queenston. Laura Secord Homestead, just below Brock's Monument at Queenston and Partition Streets. S.O. Home of Canadian heroine; restored and furnished with an excellent collection of Upper Canadian furniture.

Sault Ste. Marie. Ermatinger House, 831 Queen Street East. S.O. Built in 1814, this is the oldest house in northern Ontario. Restored and furnished in period.

Toronto. Campbell House, 160 Queen Street West. A.Y. Beautiful colonial brick house, restored and furnished in period.

Colborne Lodge, High Park. A.Y. Attractive Regency style house (haunted)—rich with antiques including Canada's first indoor toilet.

Cornell House, Thomson Memorial Park, Brimley Road and Lawrence Avenue East. S.O. Furnishings and displays dating back to 1850.

Gibson House, 5172 Yonge Street. A.Y. Perfectly restored house of the mid-1800s. Daily demonstrations of pioneer crafts.

The Grange, 317 Dundas Street West at Beverley Street. A.Y. Gentleman's residence of the 1840s, immaculately restored.

Mackenzie House, 82 Bond Street. A.Y. Home of William Lyon Mackenzie. Furnishings are authentic 1800s, and there are many mementos of Mackenzie's colourful life.

Flea Markets

It is a far cry from those days back in the 1960s when dealers at Aberfoyle, then Canada's only flea market, drove home every Sunday with empty trucks and full pockets — well, maybe not so full, since in those days they were glad to get $2 for a bulls-eye lamp, but at least they had the field to themselves.

Since then flea markets have sprung up like weeds. Prices have gone up and up at about the same rate that quality has gone down and down. Flea markets have become the home of cheap jack, and one must search diligently for good antiques. But they can still be found at

The armchairs in the parlour of the Mackenzie House, Black Creek Pioneer Village, Toronto, Ontario are upholstered in horsehair and are typical of the period (1867). Berlin work, a popular Victorian craft, covers the footstool.

the better markets, and a visit can be rewarding for the perceptive buyer.

The following may or may not be the better markets, but they are certainly the biggest and are listed here on the grounds that the more there are of them, the more likely you are to trip over an under-priced treasure.

At worst, they still provide the best of entertainment, which is more than can be said of all those infinitely dreary garage sales.

Aberfoyle Antique Market (near Guelph), Brock Road 46, north of Highway 401. S.O., Sundays. Each dealer has his own lock-up stall and the sheer quantity of merchandise offers a full day of good hunting.

Hamilton. Circle M Ranch, Highway 5, 4 miles west of Highway 6. A.Y., Sundays. About 150 dealers in a heterogeneous collection of buildings. Lots of old-timers and good pickings.

East Gate Mall, Highway 20 and Queenston Road, A.Y., Sundays. Over 100 dealers in covered mall. Lots of free parking.

Jordan Valley Flea Market, Highway 81. A.Y., Sundays. 50-100 dealers. Good for antiques and antique car parts.

London. Four City Flea Market, Western Fair Grounds, King Street. A.Y., Sundays. 100 dealers. Wide variety of stuff.

Millgrove Swap Meet, Highway 6 north of Highway 5. A.Y., Sundays. 60 dealers. Furniture, antiques and smallwares.

Pickering. East Metro Flea Market, Pickering Sheridan Mall, Highway 401 and Liverpool Road. A.Y., Sundays. 150-300 vendors make this a big one. Wide variety of everything.

Stittsville. Stittsville Flea Market. Seven miles west of Ottawa on old Highway 7. A.Y., Sundays. 200 dealers in four buildings. Largest in eastern Ontario.

Stouffville. Flea Market and Livestock, north of Stouffville on Highway 47. A.Y., Saturdays. sometimes as many as 400 vendors. Very popular.

Toronto. Harbourfront Antique Market, between Spadina and York Quay. A.Y., Sundays. 150-175 dealers. Good selection of interesting items. Great entertainment for tourists. Free lectures on antiques every week.

Heritage Antique Market, Bayview Village Shopping Centre, Bayview and Sheppard. Second Sunday each month, September to May. Fifty selected dealers from all over Ontario.

PRINCE EDWARD ISLAND

Museums

Alberton. Alberton Museum, Poplar Street. S.O. Period rooms with early furniture.

Bonshaw. Car Life Museum, Trans-Canada Highway. S.O. Old cars, tractors and farm equipment.

Charlottetown. Beaconsfield, 2 Kent Street. A.Y. Former home of Island shipbuilder, now headquarters for the Prince Edward Island Heritage Foundation.

Elmira. Elmira Railway Station, Route K6A, 10 miles east of Souris. S.O. Restored station housing railroad memorabilia.

Long River. Long River Old Mill Museum, off Route 234. Extensive display of many antique items.

Miscouche. Acadian Museum of Prince Edward Island, Route 2 West. S.O. Acadian artifacts back to 1755.

Montague. Garden of the Gulf Museum, 6 Main Street. S.O. Domestic artifacts and gun collection.

Murray Harbour. Log Cabin Museum, Route 18A. S.O. Outstanding collection of antiques going back 200 years.

An array of lighting devices, early to late, in the Log Cabin Museum, Murray Harbour, P.E.I. A lamp on a bracket hangs at the upper left, with a reflector behind it. There is a pierced tin candle lantern in the centre of the second shelf from the top. A glass lantern is on the shelf directly above it.

The Log Cabin Museum, Murray Harbour, P.E.I. also houses a collection of 19th and 20th century stoneware and china.

O'Leary. O'Leary Museum, Centennial Park. S.O. Log barn featuring pioneer furniture.

Port Hill. Green Park, Route 12, 20 miles west of Summerside. S.O. Museum of early shipbuilding in a restored 1865 home.

South Rustico. Jumpin' Jack's Museum, off Route 6 on Route 242. S.O. Authentic 19th century store.

Pioneer Villages

Belfast. Lord Selkirk Pioneer Settlement, off Trans-Canada Highway at Eldon. S.O. Located in historic forest where Selkirk settlers actually landed in 1803.

Mont Carmel. Acadian Pioneer Village, on Route 11, Lady Slipper Drive. S.O. Reproduction of early Acadian settlement.

York. Jewell's Pioneer Village, Route 25. S.O. circa 1869 village, restored. Good collection of antique glass.

Historic Parks

Freetown. Scales Pond Historic Park, on Route 109, 3 miles from Kinkora. S.O. Vintage electrical items in the restored Rogers Homestead.

Houses

Cavendish. Anne of Green Gables House, Highway 6, ¼ mile west of the main Cavendish intersection. S.O. Farm home famous as setting for Anne of Green Gables.

French River. Anne's House of Dreams, Route 20. S.O. Depicts the home of Anne and Gilbert. Turn-of-century furniture.

New London. L.M. Montgomery Birthplace. S.O. Birthplace of author of *Anne of Green Gables* with many personal mementos.

Strathgartney. Strathgartney Homestead, Trans-Canada Highway between Bonshaw and New Haven. S.O. Authentic period decor and original furnishings grace every room in this mid 19th century Landlord's Homestead — the whole thing set in a 500 acre estate.

QUEBEC

Museums

Arthabasca. Laurier Museum, 16 rue Laurier ouest. A.Y. Victorian mansion (1876), early home of Sir Wilfrid Laurier and the place he retired to until his death in 1919. Furnished in period with many Laurier mementos.

Beebe. Beebe Museum, 110 rue Main. S.O. Fine collection of Victoriana — furniture, silverware, porcelain and musical instruments.

Chicoutimi. Saguenay-Lac-St-Jean Museum, 534 rue Jacques Cartier est. A.Y. Traditional Quebec arts, especially silverware.

Coaticook. Beaulne Museum, 96 rue Union. A.Y. Unique collection of Victorian textiles, carpet and costumes.

Eaton. Comte de Compton Museum. S.O. Antiques of early 19th century housed in two restored buildings.

Gaspe. Regional Museum, Pointe Jacques Cartier. A.Y. Displays and artifacts depicting the early days of French, English, Scottish and Irish immigration.

The dining room in the Laurier Museum, Arthabasca, Quebec. The Eastlake style chairs are upholstered in horsehair, and the sideboards are typical of fine factory furniture of the late 19th century.

The study in Le Chateau de Ramezay, Montreal, Quebec. On the table are quill pens, an inkwell and the governor's file box, which has concealed compartments. The chandelier is brass.

The salle de Nantes in Le Chateau de Ramezay, Montreal, Quebec. In the foreground is a backgammon table. The panelling is mahogany and was originally in the offices of the Compagnie des Indes de France in Nantes, France.

Iles-de-la-Madeleine. Marine Museum, Havre Aubert. S.O. Historic marine artifacts and maps.

L'Islet-sur-Mer. Bernier Maritime Museum. A.Y. Exceptional collection of marine artifacts.

Joliette. Joliette Museum, 145 rue Wilfrid-Corbeil. A.Y. Unique collection of early religious art, silverware and furniture.

Knowlton. Comte de Brome Historic Museum, Route du Bord de l'eau. S.O. Pioneer and Victorian furniture.

Lac-a-la-Croix. Museum, 301 rue Saint Paul. A.Y. Collection of regional furniture, ceramics and other antiques.

Longueuil. Electrical History Museum, 440 chemin de Chambly. A.Y. Collection of early electrical equipment.

Melbourne. Comte de Richmond Museum, rue Main sud. S.O. Restored pioneer home evoking history of Loyalists and early settlers.

Montreal. Ile-Ste-Helene Museum. A.Y. Extensive collection of early Canadian firearms and pre-1800 maps.

McCord Museum, 690 rue Sherbrooke ouest. A.Y. One of the largest collections of early Canadian costumes as well as the famous collection of Notman photographs.

La Pocatiere. Museum, 100 avenue Painchaud. A.Y. Turn of the century domestic artifacts.

Quebec City. Quebec Museum, Parc des Champs de bataille. A.Y. Collection depicts widest spectrum of Quebec culture.

Quebec Seminary Museum, 6 rue de l'Universite. A.Y. Remarkable collection of Canadian religious art, fine silverware, medallions and furniture.

Ursuline Museum, 12 rue Donnacona. A.Y. Early French Canadian furniture, silverware and paintings.

Sabrevois. Honore-Mercier Museum. Restored early 19th century farmhouse complete with original furnishings.

Saint-Constant. Canadian Railway Museum, 122A rue Saint-Pierre. S.O. One of the most important collections of railway memorabilia in North America.

Stanbridge East. Missisquoi Museum, 2 rue River. S.O. Exhibition in three buildings reconstructs village life in the early 1800s.

Trois-Rivieres. Pierre Boucher Museum, 858 rue Laviolette. A.Y. Permanent collection of period artifacts evoking religious history of the region.

Vaudreuil. Vaudreuil Historic Museum, 431 boulevard Roche. A.Y. Fine collection of early Quebec folk art in an old schoolhouse.

Ville-de-la-Baie. Mgr Doufour Museum, 3322 Blvd. de la Grande-Baie. A.Y. History of the district. Good collection of early furniture.

Pioneer Villages

Drummondville. Le village quebecois d'antan (The Quebec Village of Yesteryear).

Rawdon. The Earl Moore's Canadiana village, Route du Lac Morgan, Routes 125 and 337.

Sainte-Adele. Le Village De Seraphin, Montee-a-Seraphin, Route 117.

Houses

Chomedy. Andre-Benjamin Papineau House, 5475 boulevard Saint-Martin ouest. A.Y. Home of Andre Papineau, built in 1818, fully restored in 1976.

Montreal. Chateau Defresne, boul. Pie IX et rue Sherbrooke. A.Y. superbly restored Victorian mansion filled with early Quebec furniture and ceramics.

Chateau de Ramezay Museum, 280 rue Notre-Dame est. A.Y. Reconstructed 1705 residence of former Governor of Montreal. Now houses a unique collection of Quebec artifacts of the 18th century.

The grand facade of Le Chateau Defresne Montreal, Quebec.

SASKATCHEWAN

Museums

There are four Saskatchewan Western Development Museums designed to preserve the history of the surveying and settling of the Canadian West. Each museum has its own theme.

Moose Jaw. The Story of Transportation, 1770 Hamilton Drive, junction of Highways 1 and 2. A.Y.

North Battleford. The Story of Agriculture, junction of Highways 40 and 5 East. A.Y.

Saskatoon. The Integrated Story of Western Development, 2610 Lorne Avenue South. A.Y.

Yorkton. The Story of the People, Highway 14 west on the Yellowhead. A.Y.

Historic Parks

Battleford. National Historic Park, Battleford. A.Y. Five historic buildings, four of which are located inside a reconstructed stockade. The Commanding Officer's House has been refurnished in the style of the 1870s.

Farwell Post in Saskatchewan's Cypress Hills. Destroyed by fire in 1873, the building was rebuilt in 1967 and restored and refurnished to its 1873 form.

Fort Walsh. National Historic Park, 34 miles southwest of Maple Creek in Cypress Hills. A.Y. Farwell's and Solomon's Trading Posts restored and furnished to the 1873 period.

ANTIQUE SHOWS

They come and go, but the following list gives some of the more permanent features on the map of Canadian antiques.

January *Brampton, Ontario.* Heritage Show at Shopper's World Shopping Centre.
Mississauga, Ontario. Nostalgia Show at Square One Shopping Centre.
New Minas, Nova Scotia. Heritage Show at Zeller's Country Fair.

February *Montreal, Quebec.* Horizon Show at Place Vertu.
Ottawa, Ontario. Chateau Antiques Show at the Chateau Laurier.
Ottawa, Ontario. Yesteryear Heritage Fair at the Nepean Sportsplex.

March *London, Ontario.* Horizon Antique Show at Westmount Mall.
Mississauga, Ontario. Spring Nostalgia-Rama at the Fairgrounds.
Toronto, Ontario. Horizon Show at the Harbour Castle Hilton.
Waterloo, Ontario. Horizon Show at the Conestoga Mall.

April *Bowmanville, Ontario.* April Antiques and Folk Art Show, Flying Dutchman Hotel.
Elmira, Ontario. Maple Sugar Festival Antique Show, Pari-Mutual Building.

Montreal, Quebec. Women's Service Club Show at Montreal West Presbyterian Church.
Ottawa, Ontario. Bytown Bottle Club Show at the Nepean Sportsplex.
Thornhill, Ontario. Tool Show at York Farmer's Market.
Truro, Nova Scotia. Heritage Show at Truro Mall.
Vancouver, British Columbia. Horizon Show at the Richmond Centre.

May

Guelph, Ontario. Annual Antique Show at Centennial Arena.
Mississauga, Ontario. Giant TOREX show at the International Centre.
Red Deer, Alberta. Horizon Show at Parkland Mall.
Saskatoon, Saskatchewan. Horizon Show at Mid-Town Mall.
Winnipeg, Manitoba. Horizon Show at Unicity Fashion Square.

June

Mississauga, Ontario. Summer Nostalgia-rama at the Fairgrounds.
St. Catharines, Ontario. Horizon Show at the Pen Centre.

July

Calgary, Alberta. Horizon Show at the South Centre.
Edmonton, Alberta. Horizon Show at the Londonderry Mall.
Lennoxville, Quebec. Lennoxville Antique Show, Bishop's University.
Vancouver, British Columbia. Horizon Show at the Lougheed Mall.

Winnipeg, Manitoba. Horizon Show at the St. Vital Centre.

August

Charlottetown, Prince Edward Island. Antikes at the Ole Skool Show at Royalty Mall.
Huntsville, Ontario. Muskoka Pioneer Village Market Day.
Winnipeg, Manitoba. Brewery Memorabilia Show.

September

Edmonton, Alberta. Heritage Show at Eastgate Mall.
Montreal, Quebec. IODE Antique Show at the Town Hall.
Toronto, Ontario. Heritage Antique Market at Bayview Village Shopping Centre. Monthly, from September to May.

October

Halifax, Nova Scotia. Antikes at the Ole Skool Show at Halifax Shopping Centre.
Kingston, Ontario. Kingston Antique and Art Show, Olympic Centre (sometimes held in September).
Mississauga, Ontario. Giant TOREX Show at the International Centre.
Thornhill, Ontario. Fall Tool Show at York Farmer's Market.

November

Moncton, New Brunswick. Antikes at the Ole Skool Show at the Moncton Hall.

December

Montreal, Quebec. Winter Antique Show at Place Bonaventure.

Clubs and Associations

GENERAL

Antikes at the Ole Skool
Meductic, New Brunswick EOH 1LO

The main activity is the organization of antique shows in all parts of the Maritimes. Contact the above address (or phone 1-506-272-2179) for current dates and locations.

Diggers Club
P. O. Box 942
Chemainus, British Columbia VOK 1KO

According to them, "Now that good digging sites have become a rarity, we spend our time digging for antiques at flea markets, garage sales and shows, etc. We are mostly interested in bottles and country store collectibles."

Mid-Island Collectors Club
c/o Jeanne Elder
2834 Wentworth Road
Courtenay, British Columbia V9N 6B6

Jeanne Elder says, "Our members collect a great variety of things — old toys, dolls, pharmacy items, dairy items, soda syphons, green glass, button hooks, old kitchen utensils, R.S. Prussia, etc., etc. We publish a regular newsletter and hold an annual show and sale."

"I'm a Collector" Club
P. O. Box 5192
Whitehorse, Yukon Territory Y1A 4S3

Open to anyone who collects anything. They encourage collectors with similar interests to get together via their monthly newsletter which includes free advertising for members.

GLASS

The Canadian Carnival Glass Association
P. O. Box 202
Ancaster, Ontario L9G 3L4

Membership is at present $5.00 a year, and they have about 150 active members across Canada.

Glasfax
906A Meadow Woods Road
Mississauga, Ontario L5J 2S9

One of several branches in Ontario for people interested in the history and collecting of early Canadian pressed glass. Activities consist mainly in meetings addressed by well-informed guest speakers.

Old Time Bottle Club of British Columbia
P. O. Box 77154
Vancouver, British Columbia V5R 5T4

A club for people interested in the history and collecting of British Columbia bottles. They issue a monthly newsletter with swap and show information.

The Prairie Depression Glass Club
23 Park Road North
Grimsby, Ontario L3M 2P2

The name of the club dates back to 1976, when Loreen Holowaychuk of Lanigan, Saskatchewan, and 17 other people got together to form an association of shared interest. Today, there are over 250 members in all parts of the country who, for a trivial fee, receive a regular, information-packed newsletter with what amounts to a running price guide.

FURNITURE

Miniature Enthusiasts of Toronto
171 Homewood Avenue
Willowdale, Ontario M2M 1K4

This is the contact address for the 15 clubs in various parts of Canada devoted to collecting and making miniatures of all kinds — with particular emphasis on miniature furniture.

BOOKS, PRINTS AND MAPS

The American Society of Bookplate Collectors and Designers
#F, 605 N. Stonemand Avenue
Alhambra, California 91801

COLLECTIBLES

British Columbia Historical Arms Collectors
P. O. Box 80583
Burnaby, British Columbia V5H 3X9

The Canadian Association of Token Collectors
10 Wesanford Place
Hamilton, Ontario L8P 1N6

They publish a bi-monthly newsletter with articles and swap-list.

Canadian Society of Military Medals and Insignia
P. O. Box 1263
Guelph, Ontario N1H 6N6

They publish a journal.

The Canadian Vintage Wireless Association
Ontario: 197 Humberside Avenue
Toronto, Ontario M6P 1K7

Quebec: 75 Parkdale Avenue
Pointe Claire, Quebec H9R 3Y6

Alberta: 19 Leon Place
St. Albert, Alberta T8N 1X6

Members receive a quarterly publication called *The Cat's Whisker* devoted to news and views on early radio receivers and other equipment.

Military Collectors Club of Canada
646 Irwin Avenue
Newmarket, Ontario L3Y 5A2

They publish a journal.

The Toronto Postcard Club
c/o Glen Gardiner
59 Cedar Drive
Scarborough, Ontario M1J 3E9

The club was founded in 1977 by Bob McEvilla. They meet twice a month to talk about such things as election cards, leap-year cards, automotive-related cards and winter sports cards — just a few of the more obscure sub-sections of the hobby. They publish a newsletter.

The Vancouver Postcard Club
c/o Stan Stewardson
229 Regina Street
New Westminster, British Columbia V3L 1S7

The club meets once a month to discuss topics of mutual interest.

MISCELLANEOUS

The British Columbia Spoon Club
7671 Minoru Gate
Richmond, British Columbia V6Y 1R8

Devoted to the complexities of spoon collecting. Local membership meets regularly and sponsors spoon shows. Their publication, *Input*, reaches out-of-town members in all parts of Canada.

Canadian Chapter of the American Bell Association
R. R. 2
Binbrook, Ontario L0R 1C0

This is the contact point for branches in all parts of Canada. They publish a monthly newsletter and organize shows.

The Canadian Knife Collectors Club
25 Raven Lane
Pickering, Ontario L1V 3C7

Collectors share news on the Canadian knife scene. They sponsor shows and issue annual limited edition knives.

The Heraldry Society of Canada
125 Lakeway Drive
Ottawa, Ontario K1L 5A9

The International Music Box Society
P. O. Box 202
Route 3
Morgantown, Indiana 46160

The National Association of Watch and Clock Collectors
Chapter 33: Peter Buckley, Secretary
    6 Tepee Court
    Willowdale, Ontario M2J 3A9
Chapter 92: Harold Leach, Secretary
    247 Halls Mill Road
    London, Ontario N6K 2L3
Chapter 111: Peter Bomford, Secretary
    14 Kinnear Street
    Ottawa, Ontario K1Y 3R4

Victoria Historic Fishing Tackle Club
189 Beach Avenue
Victoria, British Columbia V8S 2L6

Members meet four times a year and organize special events related to increasing their knowledge and appreciation of such old fishing tackle as reels, rods and lures, and old books.

Bibliography

GLASS

Doros, Paul E. *The Tiffany Collection.* Norfolk, VA: Chrysler Museum at Norfolk, 1977.

Florence, Gene. *The Collector's Encyclopedia of Depression Glass.* Paducah, KY: Collector Books, 1977.

Gardner, Paul F. *The Glass of Frederick Carder.* New York: Crown Publishers, 1971.

Hartung, Marion T. *Carnival Glass in Colour.* Des Moines: Wallace Homestead, n.d. *Northwood Pattern Glass.* Des Moines: Wallace Homestead, n.d.

Hotchkiss, John F. *Carder's Steuben Glass.* Pittsford, NY: Privately Printed, 1964.

Kaellgren, C. Peter, ed. *A Gather of Glass: Glass Through the Ages in the Royal Ontario Museum.* Toronto: The Royal Ontario Museum, 1977.

Klamkin, Marian. *The Collector's Guide to Depression Glass.* New York: Hawthorn Books, 1973.

Koch, Robert. *Louis C. Tiffany's Glass, Bronzes and Lamps: A Complete Collector's Guide.* New York: Crown Publishers, 1971.

Roden's Cut Glass Catalogue Reprint. Peterborough, Ont.: Clock House, 1974.

Spence, Hilda, and Kelvin Spence. *A Guide to Early Canadian Glass.* Toronto: Longmans Canada, 1966.

Stevens, Gerald. *Early Canadian Glass.* Toronto: Ryerson Press, 1960.

Unitt, Doris J. and Peter Unitt. *Treasury of Canadian Glass.* Peterborough, Ont.: Clock House, 1969.

Weatherman, Hazel Marie. *Coloured Glassware of the Depression Era.* Bks. I-II. Ozark, MO: Privately Printed, 1977, 1978.

CERAMICS

Antonelli, Marylu and Jack Forbes. *Pottery in Alberta: The Long Tradition.* Edmonton: University of Alberta Press, 1978.

Collard, Elizabeth. *Nineteenth-Century Pottery and Porcelain in Canada.* Montreal: McGill University Press, 1967.

Finlayson, R.W. *Portneuf Pottery and Other Early Wares.* Toronto: Longmans Canada, 1972.

Godden, Geoffrey A. *Encyclopedia of British Pottery and Porcelain Marks.* London: Barrie & Jenkins, 1970.

Goss Heraldic (magazine and price guide), ed. Nicholas Pine. 62 Murray Road, Horndean, Portsmouth, Hantshire, P01 9JL, England.

Newlands, David L. *Early Ontario Potters: Their Craft and Trade.* Toronto: McGraw-Hill Ryerson, 1979.

Symonds, Richard and Jean Symonds. *Medalta Stoneware and Pottery for Collectors.* Surrey, B.C.: Symco, 1974.

Webster, Donald Blake. *Decorated Stoneware Pottery of North America.* Rutland, VT: Charles E. Tuttle, 1971.
Early Canadian Pottery. Toronto: McClelland and Stewart, 1971.
Early Slip-Decorated Pottery in Canada. Toronto: Charles J. Musson, 1969.
The Brantford Pottery, 1849-1907. Toronto: The Royal Ontario Museum, 1968.

METALS

Barbeau, Charles Marius. *Trésor des Anciens Jésuites,* Ottawa: Queen's Printer, 1957.

Langdon, John E. *Canadian Silversmiths 1700-1900.* Toronto: Stinehour Press, 1966.
Guide to Marks on Early Canadian Silver. Toronto: Macmillan, 1940.

Traquair, Ramsay. *The Old Silver of Quebec.* Toronto: Macmillan, 1940.

Unitt, Doris, and Peter Unitt. *Canadian Silver, Silverplate and Related Glass.* Peterborough, Ont.: Clock House, 1970.

FURNITURE

Blundell, Peter S. *The Marketplace Guide to Oak Furniture.* Toronto: Thorncliffe House, 1980.
and Phil T. Dunning. *The Marketplace Guide to Victorian Furniture.* Toronto: Thorncliffe House, 1981.

Dobson, Henry and Barbara Dobson. *The Early Furniture of Ontario and the Atlantic Provinces.* Toronto: M.F. Feheley Publishers, 1974.

Ingolsfrud, Elizabeth. *All About Ontario Chairs.* Toronto: House of Grant, 1974. A well done little paperback, one of a series, the others being *All About Ontario Beds, . . .Chests, . . .Tables, . . .Cupboards,* etc.

Minhinnick, Jeanne. *At Home in Upper Canada.* Toronto: Clarke, Irwin, 1970. The cover refers to "the romance and reality of domestic life in Canada before Confederation." It goes far beyond furniture. A classic.

Musson-Nykor, Lynda, and Patricia D. Musson. *Mennonite Furniture: the Ontario Tradition in York County.* Toronto: Lorimer, 1977.

Pain, Howard. *The Heritage of Upper Canadian Furniture.* Toronto: Van Nostrand Reinhold, 1978. An encyclopedic work superbly illustrated with 1450 excellent photographs, each one carefully described. It is likely to remain the classic study for as far ahead as can be visualized.

Palardy, Jean. *The Early Furniture of French Canada.* Toronto: Macmillan of Canada, 1963. The standard work on French-Canadian furniture.

Shackleton, Philip. *The Furniture of Old Ontario.* Toronto: Macmillan of Canada, 1973.

Stevens, Gerald. *Early Ontario Furniture.* Toronto: Royal Ontario Museum, 1966.

Webster, Donald Blake. *English Canadian Furniture of the Georgian Period.* Toronto: McGraw-Hill Ryerson, 1979.

BOOKS, PRINTS AND MAPS

Bricker, Charles. *Landmarks of Mapmaking.* New York: Thomas Y. Crowell, 1976.

Hind, Arthur M. *A History of Engraving and Etching: From the Fifteenth Century to the Year 1914.* 3rd rev. ed. New York: Dover Publications, 1963. The standard work on how to identify different print-making methods.

Shulman, Morton. *Anyone Can Make Big Money Buying Art.* Toronto: Fitzhenry & Whiteside, 1977.

Spendlove, Francis St. George. *The Face of Early Canada: Pictures of Canada Which Have Helped to Make History.* Toronto: Ryerson Press, 1958. The classic volume listing most early Canadian prints.

Theberge, C.B. *Canadiana on Your Bookshelf.* Toronto: J.M. Dent, 1976.

Tooley, Ronald V. *Maps and Mapmakers.* 6th ed. New York: Crown Publishers, 1978.

COLLECTIBLES

Hogan, Bill and Pauline Hogan. *Canadian Country Store Collectables.* St. Catharines, Ont.: Privately Printed, 1979. A very good, well illustrated paperback, available from the authors at 16 Haynes Avenue, St. Catharines, Ontario L2R 3Z1.

Leibowitz, Alan. *The Record Collector's Handbook.* Edison, NJ: Everest House, 1980.

Soderbergh, Peter A. *Olde Records Price Guide: Popular and Classical Seventy-Eight RPM's 1900-1947.* Des Moines: Wallace Homestead, 1980.

MISCELLANEOUS

Barilli, Renato, *Art Nouveau.* London: Paul Hamlyn, 1969.

Bird, Michael S. *Ontario Fraktur: A Pennsylvania-German Tradition.* M.F. Feheley Publishers, 1977.

 and Terry Kobayashi. *A Splendid Harvest: Germanic Folk and Decorative Arts in Canada.* Toronto: Van Nostrand Reinhold, 1981.

Burrows, G. Edmond. *Canadian Clocks and Clockmakers.* Oshawa: Kalabi Enterprises, 1973. "Books of All Time," P.O. Box 604, Brockville, Ontario K6V 5V8, is a specialty dealer in books about clocks: collecting, repairing, history, etc.; they publish a catalogue.

Conroy, Mary. *300 Years of Canadian Quilts.* Toronto: Griffin House, 1976.

Harper, J. Russell. *A People's Art.* Toronto: University of Toronto Press, 1974.

Lesieutra, Alain. *The Spirit and Splendor of Art Deco.* New York: Paddington, 1974.

McClinton, Katherine Morrison. *Art Deco.* New York: Potter, 1972.

Mackay, James. *Childhood Antiques.* New York: Taplinger, 1976.

McKendry, Ruth. *Quilts and Other Bed Coverings in the Canadian Tradition.* Toronto: Van Nostrand Reinhold, 1979.

Mebane, John. *The Complete Book of Collecting Art Nouveau.* New York: Coward McCann, 1970.

Sloane, Eric. *A Museum of Early American Tools.* New York: Ballantine, 1964.

Warner, Glen. *Building a Print Collection: A Guide to Buying Original Prints and Photographs.* Toronto: Van Nostrand Reinhold, 1981.

Webster, Donald Blake. *Book of Canadian Antiques.* Toronto: McGraw Hill, 1974.

PERIODICALS

Antiques & Art. 2227 Granville Street, Vancouver, B.C. V6H 3G1.

Canadian Antiques & Art Review. P.O. Box 3664, Halifax South, Halifax, N.S. B3J 3K6.

Canadian Collector. 27 Carlton Street, Suite 406, Toronto, Ont. M5B 1L2.

CanadiAntiquer. R.R. #1, Hagersville, Ont. N0A 1H0.

Index